TOOLBOX FOR
YOUNG ADULT SUCCESS

KELLIE O'CALLAGHAN

PUBLISH **HER**

UCONFIDENCE: YOUNG ADULT TOOLBOX FOR SUCCESS

© Copyright 2022 Kellie O'Callaghan

ISBN: 979-8-9865220-0-5
Printed in the United States of America
First Printing: 2022

Published by Publish Her, LLC
2909 South Wayzata Boulevard
Minneapolis, MN 55405
www.publishherpress.com

Author photo by Kessel Cripe Photography

Keltan, Cael and Kessel:
I love you to infinity and beyond
—Mom

CONTENTS

INTRODUCTION

You don't know me yet, but you will by the end of this book. I am a business owner, academic coach and tutor. I am the person who prepares young adults for standardized tests like ACTs, SATs and PSATs. I support students in writing college essays and completing college applications on time. I also work as a reading coach and an ADD[1] and ADHD[2] life coach, which means I help my clients navigate challenges in life that are unique to them.

I have worked with thousands of students in college and high school. I admire and respect you and hold you in the highest regard. I have empathy[3] for you. Your life is much harder than the generations before you, mine included. You've probably been told by adults you have it easy, or how much harder it was when they were younger. I disagree. Your life is hard in different and insidious[4] ways.

See those footnotes? You'll see them throughout

---

1 Attention Deficit Disorder
2 Attention Deficit Hyperactivity Disorder
3 Compassion, warmth
4 Subtle, covert

this book. I use some less common words and phrases, but I also include words that are more common and some definitions. If the footnotes help you, use them. If not, ignore them.

Over the past 15 years, I have had the honor of working with young adults to build relationships, trust and confidence. I discovered the most important part of my job is helping others build confidence. It's a game-changer for students and my favorite thing to do. If we all have a life mission, I believe helping others build confidence is mine. This book is one of the ways I share that mission with you. I will help you accept yourself for who and where you are right now. And I will give you keys and tools to build the confidence you need to get wherever you want to go next.

I want to make a few promises to you before you commit to investing your time (your most precious commodity[5]) into this book:

- I will respect you. I don't like when anyone is condescending.[6]
- I will be kind and compassionate. This is the core of who I am.
- I will be honest and direct. I am from New York and can't help it.

---

5 Product, service
6 Superior, arrogant

- I will define the terms in this book. Clear is kind; unclear is unkind.
- I will leave gender out. This book is for humans. Period.
- I will keep it simple. I'll keep the chapters short and provide lots of examples.
- I will give practical advice and strategies. I'll focus on things you can actually control.
- I will believe in you. And I will ask you to believe in yourself.
- I will help you build confidence. After all, that is the point of the book, right?

PART ONE:
CONFIDENCE KEYS

"I hope you live a life you're proud of."

—F. Scott Fitzgerald

YOU ARE ENOUGH

When I first meet a student, I spend a good amount of time getting to know them and discovering our common ground. I've learned working together goes more smoothly when starting from a place of mutual interest, agreement and truth.

Before we dig in, I'd like you to do something. Take a few deep breaths, close your eyes and see yourself—really see yourself—for who you are in this moment. Accept the reality of who you are, right here and right now. I want you to know this: YOU ARE ENOUGH, just as you are. Now celebrate yourself and how amazing you are. Give yourself a hug, a pat on the back, a round of applause—show yourself some kindness.

To begin this journey, you must first see yourself honestly. You have to start from a place of truth to move forward in truth. You may not like everything about yourself right now. That's OK. Find one thing you do admire or like about yourself and start there. It can be small, and it can seem insignificant, but it isn't. The things you admire about yourself are your strengths. No strength is insignificant—they make up the best parts of you.

In young adulthood, some of life's most important traits often get overlooked. Students believe their GPA, test scores, athletic prowess[7] or popularity say the most about them. But who you are as a human is much more than these often fleeting[8] successes. You are made of many intangibles[9] that matter more: kindness, respect, humbleness[10], gentleness, grit, creativity, self-regulation, faith, optimism, joy.

It's understandable to overlook the intangibles. Young adults receive a steady diet of messages that the most important things in life are getting a good job, earning high grades, being a strong athlete, being popular or good looking. It can be easier to laser focus on what you've been told is crucial. Initially, many of the students I work with believe these are the keys to confidence. They are not. The keys to confidence are straightforward and internal: self-trust, self-love and self-security.

---

7 Skill, ability
8 Brief, fading
9 Indirect, indefinable
10 Modesty, humility

SELF-TRUST

The first key to confidence is self-trust. I believe in me. I know I can do this. I know I am capable. I trust myself. It can be hard to trust in yourself, but this is where confidence starts. The choice to trust yourself is 100 percent yours. Accept yourself for who and where you are right now, see where you want to go in the future, and be prepared to put in the hard work and effort to get there. It's an agreement made by you, to you, with no one else present. Confidence at its root is self-trust.

SELF-LOVE

The second key to confidence is self-love. It starts with learning to love yourself and accepting that YOU ARE ENOUGH. Stop chasing some ideal of perfection that doesn't exist. Stop pushing yourself so hard. I am not saying don't strive to improve, grow or strengthen yourself. Of course, you want to do that. You have so much of your life ahead of you! But know that your value as a human does not depend on your performance, achievements, successes or failures. And it is never dependent on your role as a child, friend, student, significant other or any other role.

One of my favorite quotes is from F. Scott Fitzgerald: "I hope you make the best of it. I hope you see things that startle you. I hope you feel things you never felt before. I hope you meet people who have a different point of view. I hope you live a life you're proud of, and if you're not, I hope you have the courage to start all over again."

Are you living a life you are proud of? I didn't ask you if you're living a life that others are proud of. I asked about you. Are you on the path toward the life you want? You are never too young, or too old, to start living the life you want.

Many people in your life are on your side. They love, respect and want what is best for you. But your job in life is not to please them, perform for them or provide a stage for them to live out their dreams. Never let anyone make you doubt that YOU ARE ENOUGH.

SELF-SECURITY

The third key to confidence is self-security. This is being secure in yourself and your abilities. You develop self-security when you stop leaning on others to feel certain, safe and secure. It's knowing deep inside you that you've got things handled and you can and will do what you set out to do. Confident people are self-secure.

When I work with students, there is often confusion between the act of confidence and actual confidence. The act of confidence is what you present to the world. Actual confidence is what you feel and believe inside. People who are acting are actually insecure on the inside. Actual confident people often appear humble and understated[11] on the outside but are internally self-secure. You can't truly know how confident any individual is; you can only know how confident they appear.

ENOUGH

When you work to build your self-trust, self-love and self-security, doubts will undoubtedly pop up. To the questions, doubts and fears that creep in, I encourage you to say ENOUGH. Learning to say ENOUGH to any negative self-talk and self-image you may have developed is really important. Life is hard enough without beating yourself up.

---

11 Discreet, low-key

Take a moment to think about a time when you were hard on yourself and the way you treated or talked to yourself. Would you treat or talk to your best friend that way? Would you treat a random stranger that way? No? Then why in the world would you do that to yourself? It stops today. Right now. As Shonda Rhimes (of "Grey's Anatomy" and "Scandal" fame) says in her book, "Year of Yes," "The cruelty with which I treated myself is no longer to be tolerated."

It is time for you to trust and love yourself as you are right now. It is time for you to acknowledge to yourself, and to the world, that you deserve respect from yourself and others.

Perhaps you do accept and respect yourself. Good for you! This is a big step in being confident. But if you sometimes struggle or need a reminder, please repeat these two statements as often as needed:

- I am ENOUGH just as I am.
- I say ENOUGH to anything that feeds my self-doubt.

JUST BE

I have certain "momisms." Your parents probably do too. You know, the phrases they repeat so often they make you roll your eyes or groan and say, "I know, Mom!" When my kids were around 10 years old, I started saying, "Never stop being to start seeming." Let's unpack this.

Do you remember being 10 years old? Go back there in your mind right now. Think about all the things you loved to do, discuss and share. Do you remember not caring so much about what others thought or wanted? Think about what you were really interested in and passionate about back then, what you wanted to be or do before the world made you think it was unrealistic or that you needed to be quiet.

Kids around that age are curious, open, honest, direct, hopeful, fearless and just want adults to engage in their world with them. They simply share what they feel and know and hope you will be interested. I've met kids who are excited about frogs, fairies, astronauts, Harry Potter, ancient Rome, art, paint ball, brains, drums, word origins, role playing, reading, rockets, physics, writing and more.

Somewhere along the way, as kids get older, they lose touch with their inner 10-year-old and the things that once lit them up. Do you remember loving something so much you wanted to do it all the time and assumed everyone else did too? Do you remember that sacred time when you were truly being you? Before the world, social media, or your friends told you who or how to be? Or rather, who or how not to be anymore because it wasn't cool, acceptable, realistic or interesting? So you stopped being simply and truly you. This was when you stopped "being" to start "seeming."

It was in those moments, when you gave up parts of yourself in order to fit in with certain people or surroundings, that your confidence began to wane.[12] When you started putting others' expectations, demands and desires above your own, you began sacrificing your self-trust on the altar of fitting in.

It's not all bad to limit yourself, your interests and your desires to a certain extent. In fact, it's often necessary for the greater good. Have you ever been in

12 Fade, disappear

a classroom where kids just talk about whatever they want for however long they want? It can be a challenge to get anything done. We all make compromises to be part of a community. This is needed and can be good. What's not good or OK is forcing yourself into a box to "seem" like everyone else.

Children and young adults (and even adults) are expected to adapt, limit and change to fit into certain roles, expectations and cultural norms. I believe this has led to a confidence crisis. You young adults believe the lie that you are not ENOUGH. You believe that you will never measure up to society's standards of perfection.

Perfection does not exist and is unattainable. This is important, so I will say it again: Perfection does not exist and is unattainable. Those who seem perfect on the outside often feel like impostors on the inside. They worry they'll be discovered as a fraud. It is simply not possible to achieve all the ideals society sets forth as perfection. How do you get past this? Forget about "seeming" and get back to "being." Find peace with being yourself. Start loving and accepting yourself as you are right now. Be who you are openly, honestly, freely and proudly.

Why spend your life chasing a figment[13] of reality

---

13 Illusion, fantasy

or pretending to be someone else? Live your life like that interesting, curious, energetic, honest person you were at 10, before the world told you who you should be instead. Share what lights you up. That light is uniquely yours. Let it shine so brightly that everyone can see it. Never let anyone douse[14] your flame. You may have been taught to be humble or grateful or follow the rules, but don't let the rules make you lose sight of yourself and your strengths.

---

14 Cover, extinguish

HERO

Everyone loves a good story—one where the hero faces the obstacles thrown their way, overcomes them and gets their happy ending. This is the plot line of many great movies, books and lives. This is a reminder to you: Your story is a hero's journey, and you are the hero.

As the story of your life unfolds, don't forget that you are the author and the narrator. Tell your story in a positive light. Tell it as if the ending is already figured out—as if you have done the work, achieved your goals, completed your journey, and not only survived but thrived. Be confident that your story is one that's interesting enough to make into a blockbuster movie. Don't cede[15] your plot line to anyone. Would you let your friends put you in a weird "choose your own adventure" life, with a character they decide best fits you and an ending they want to happen? Heck

---

15 Surrender, abandon

no! This is your story; you get to live it the way you want to.

Picture your favorite tale: "Percy Jackson," "Harry Potter," "Hunger Games," "Star Wars," "Anne of Green Gables," "Rocky," "James Bond," "Lord of the Rings," "Divergent," "Avengers." Do you know what most of the heroes in these stories have in common? They did not start their journeys with confidence. Rather, the heroes started with their unique strengths and developed confidence along the way.

Hermione Granger from "Harry Potter" is one of my favorite examples of a strong hero. (Yes, I am a nerdy bookworm!) Hermione works from her strengths of intelligence and research, which is why I like her. She also develops into an unexpectedly tough hero in ways that are not so cerebral.[16] She trusts herself, even and especially when others do not believe in or trust her.

Ron Weasley's self-confidence takes longer to develop. His hero's journey is slower and twistier because he cares so deeply about what everyone around him thinks. Ron is often too scared to trust himself without the support and encouragement of others. Can you relate? Ron gets there in the end, but he has to work through self-doubt as he battles to discover

---

16 Analytical, intellectual

himself. For much of the story, Ron never seems quite sure what his strengths are. Hermione grows more quickly into a hero than Ron, not because she is more of one, but because she leads with her strengths and does not give a whit[17] what anyone else thinks about her intelligence. Everyone could take a lesson from Hermione.

Samwise Gamgee from "The Lord of the Rings" is one of the most loyal characters in literature or film. His dependability is unparalleled and his greatest strength. According to JRR Tolkien, Samwise is the true hero because he's happy to let Frodo take the credit. He exudes[18] humble confidence and is unassuming. He is driven by loyalty, love and the simple pleasures of life. Sam knows his strengths and weaknesses and works from them. His confidence is founded in his knowledge, devotion and contentment. Samwise never claims to be a hero and therefore does not succumb to the temptation of the One Ring.

These examples are not typical heroes. They may even be viewed as sidekicks. There are many heroes who don't wear capes or have their name in the title. You might see yourself in some of these sidekicks. It's common to relate to others you see as similar to you. But don't undersell yourself or your value. Never

---

17 Bit, iota
18 Radiates, transmits

forget: You are the main character in your story, and yours is a hero's journey.

The story you tell matters. Your words matter. You could make your story a victim's journey. You could turn yourself into a villain—in your own story, or someone else's. You could be your own worst enemy. You can do all of that with just words. People come to trust and believe words. Choose them wisely. When you do, tap into your self-trust, self-love and self-security. Speak about yourself the way you would a loved one—a person you respect and admire. Just as you would encourage loved ones to speak positively about themselves, do the same for yourself.

QUARTERBACK

When I work with a student, I ask about their passions, hobbies and activities. To some, this is surprising. They wonder what it has to do with test prep or life coaching. It has everything to do with it! Some of your most formative experiences occur in the hours spent outside of the classroom. You are a whole person with varied interests, abilities, challenges and talents. You have been shaped by your experiences and have grown into the person you are today.

I have been blessed with the opportunity to work with many athletes. Perhaps this is because I am more of a coach than a traditional teacher. My style seems to gel[19] with athletes, and they recommend me to one another. As a result, I have developed an arsenal[20] of sports analogies and lessons over the past decade. Some are groaners (think bad dad jokes), some fall completely short and a few have had a lasting impact. Football is often my go-to analogy[21] source.

---

19 Mix, combine
20 Supply, stock
21 Comparison, metaphor

QUARTERBACK

You are the quarterback of your life. You are an authority and expert on you. Don't give anyone else responsibility for or control over making the calls in your life. You need to touch the ball on every offensive play. Call the signals to your team. Know when to run, when to throw and when to call an audible.[22] Have the confidence of an NFL quarterback.

Great quarterbacks are not born; they are made. They are coached, they train and they work harder than most humans think they are capable of. Quarterbacks push themselves every day. They surround themselves with phenomenal coaches and great teammates and are responsible for bringing everyone together to make plays work. Be your own quarterback.

Quarterbacks cannot win football games alone. They may call and run the plays, but they have a whole team supporting them and running the ball and interference for them. You also need a support system in your confidence journey—individuals on your team who each play a special role.

---

22 Verbal change in play after the huddle and before the snap

OFFENSIVE LINE

An offensive line is made up of tackles, guards and centers. These are your go-to teammates who literally[23] throw down and take hits for you. They help you accomplish your goals. They don't always get the credit they deserve and tend to fly under the radar to everyone except the quarterback. To the quarterback, they are an irreplaceable line of protection. There's a reason they are called the offensive line and not the defensive line. It's because they are always advancing the ball (supporting your goals), and they hate losing ground. Their goals are forward momentum and protecting the quarterback at all costs.

While your confidence is within you, your offensive line helps you recognize and build it. They help protect you from sacks[24], injuries and defeat. Without them, life would be a lot more difficult.

Who is your offensive line? Who will stand up for you, defend you in your absence and help you move forward? Everyone needs an offensive line. Your offense need to be strong, share your goals and want you to succeed.

---

23 Actually, truly
24 Tackled behind the line of scrimmage before throwing a pass

RECEIVERS AND BACKS

These are the teammates who always have your back. They receive your passes, take your hand-offs and run as fast and far as they can. Like the offensive line, they help you reach your goals. Receivers and backs are quick, adaptable and very dependable. They learn your tells. They can read you and know you almost as well as you know yourself. They believe in you, sometimes more than you believe in yourself. When your confidence is low, they help keep it high. Working together, you can make some amazing winning plays.

DEFENSE

Your defensive teams help surround the opposition. They stop attacks against your goal and prevent your opponents from scoring against you. The main mission of the defense is containment, standing strong and getting possession of the ball back to you as fast and with as little damage as possible. Your defensive team helps boost your confidence as well. They constantly make sure you have control of the ball. Though you're not on the field at the same time, they are just as critical to your success and confidence as your offensive line.

SPECIAL TEAMS

Special teams join the game during unique but critical junctures.[25] They help you accomplish very specific tasks and do them well. You call them the moment you are down, knowing they can pick you right back up. They seem to always know just what to say or do to get you and the game back on track.

While sometimes overlooked and viewed as playing a tiny role, as the quarterback you know how essential they really are to you and your success. You have complete faith in these members of your team because they have a history of executing their role with excellence every time.

COACHES

Coaches are essential to every good team. They tend to develop a close relationship with the quarterback. A coach's goal is to train, support and encourage you and then watch you shine. Ultimately, coaches help you become the best version of yourself. We are always on your side, working endlessly behind the scenes to assist you in whatever way we can.

Truth be told, a coach may not always be your

---

25 Moments, stages

favorite person. That is OK. Coaches don't mind if you like us most when you win the Superbowl. We know what our job is and how to execute it despite any protests. We lift you up and help you build confidence. A coach reminds you how good you are and pushes you to be even better. Coaches are honest, direct, tough and compassionate. Coaches know your greatest challenges and work from your greatest strengths.

Together, coaches and quarterbacks strategize, plan and run practices. Then on game day, your coach trusts and believes in you to execute and shine. The proudest days of a coach's life are when we watch you risk it all, leave it all on the field and confidently show up as yourself. Even if the outcome isn't exactly as planned, nothing makes us prouder.

CHEERLEADERS AND FANS

Cheerleaders and fans are an important part of your team. You need people who jump up and down for joy and root for you. They help boost your confidence in your most vulnerable moments. When the odds are stacked against you, or you feel like throwing in the towel, cheerleaders and fans go all-in—with their voices, bodies and hearts. They keep the faith, often long after others are convinced you can't win. They believe in you and don't care if you win or lose. They are your confidence keepers when it seems like all hope is lost.

Listen to and believe what your cheerleaders and fans say about you. Let them buoy[26] you and rally your confidence. And don't forget to thank them for their encouragement.

BUILD YOUR TEAM

Take a moment to think about your team. It may be big, small or not even exist yet. The size of your team doesn't matter—heart and unity do. If you have a small but effective team, that's great. If you don't have one, start developing your team today. Look for the people who can play these roles in your life.

Maybe your team exists but there are people on it who don't belong there because they don't lift you up or share your goals. Make sure everyone deserves a spot on your team. Don't allow others to control or live vicariously[27] through you.

Confidence is about self-love, self-trust and self-security, and it is also about surrounding yourself with people who help build you up. Everyone needs others

---

26 Uplift, boost
27 Indirectly, secondarily

who will fight for them, both on the gridiron[28] and off. When you lack confidence, trust the confidence of those around you and allow it to help propel you forward.

Support and lean on your team, but always remember, you are the quarterback of your life. Even with the support of others, you are responsible for making and controlling the calls. Stay focused on your goals. Be the awesome quarterback I know you can be!

---

28 Field, stadium

BOUNDARIES

There are entire books written about boundaries. Two that I recommend are "Rising Strong" by Dr. Brené Brown and "Set Boundaries, Find Peace" by Nedra Glover Tawwab.

In the simplest terms, boundaries come down to two clearly communicated lists: what is OK and what is not OK. There are many types of boundaries, and every day you probably bump up against these limits in some way. Laws are boundaries. Rules are boundaries. Common decency can be viewed as a boundary. Boundaries are not inherently bad or good; they are simply clear demarcations[29] of behavior. Boundaries tell you where the lines are drawn in the sand, and they let others know where your lines are.

Some people struggle with boundaries more than others. If you are someone who has trouble following or respecting boundaries, it is time to make a change. If it's hard for you to create clear boundaries for yourself,

---

29 Limits, distinctions

it is time to make a change. While some people can struggle in both areas, it is more likely your challenge is pushing boundaries.

Young adults often find themselves in the boundary-pushing realm of life. You are trying to find and make your own way. Sometimes it might feel like you have to push against every limit to see if it stands firm or not. This pushing allows you to discover which boundaries are cast in cement and which ones are malleable.[30]

Here's an analogy that I hope illustrates boundaries and how it might feel to those whose boundaries you are pushing:

My kids were all swimmers. Swimmers perform flip turns over and over again. It's when they accelerate toward the pool wall, flip over at full speed, push off the wall and propel themselves in the opposite direction. Swimmers are strong and powerful; they push off with ferocity[31] in order to go in the opposite direction as fast and as far as possible.

While young adults are like swimmers, parents (especially moms) are like pool walls. We are secure, grounded, firm and unmoving. As you head our way, you need to trust that we will be exactly where we promised and do exactly what we are supposed to do. You need to count on it enough to hurl yourself toward

---

30 Flexible, adaptable
31 Wildness, ferociousness

a solid wall of cement and tile. You need to be secure in the fact that you will get the boost you need from your parent (pushing off the pool wall) in order to head toward your goal.

Like swimmers, you young adults are not always gentle in your approach. You can be even harsher with your push off. The older and stronger you get, the harder you might push the wall. It's understandable. This is the way you've learned to move forward. It's what helps you gather courage and confidence to keep going.

Solid boundaries are clear end markers. They can be counted on. Pool walls are strong and stand the test of time against constant pushing. Parents do too.

Contrast swimming in a pool to jumping into the middle of the ocean where there are no clear boundaries. At first, it might feel beautiful, endless and freeing. Then, with no land in sight and no life vest, you may realize you have no idea what to do next. You'd probably begin to worry how long you can swim or stay afloat. A life without boundaries can feel like being in the ocean with no clear way out.

Now, imagine there is another person with you in the ocean. Let's say the two of you agree you need to get to land and strategize how to reach your goal.

You agree on a plan of action and start to work as a team. But what if you can't agree? Some people in this scenario might hold onto the other person to stay afloat. A person without boundaries might allow it. Would you play the role of a life preserver for someone else while lost at sea with no land in sight? Someone with weak or nonexistent boundaries could find themselves in this position. And a person with no respect for boundaries might take full advantage of it.

Take a moment to think about the role of boundaries in your life, both good and bad. Some limits are healthy for us. Some boundary-pushing is OK and good for growth—as long as it is respectful. Boundaries don't allow for or justify disrespect or abuse.

It may seem like boundaries are for and about everyone else. But boundaries are not about others as much as they are about you. They are the limits of what is and is not acceptable for you. In order for a boundary to mean anything, it has to be clear, obvious and solid, like the pool wall. Start noticing, creating and clearly communicating your boundaries. Start noticing and asking about other people's boundaries. Use boundaries to propel you forward, not to pull someone else under. Boundaries don't mean being selfish. They are critical to building self-respect, self-love, self-trust and self-security—the foundations of confidence.

EMPATHY

Developing confidence requires developing empathy and surrounding yourself with others who have empathy as well.

Do you have a friend you call when you're heading into a tailspin? Odds are, that friend is empathetic. This is the friend who doesn't tell you to "Buck up, buckaroo" or "Rub some dirt on it," when times are hard. They don't pretend everything is peachy-keen.[32] They don't tell you, "Turn that frown upside down." More than likely, this person sits with you in your pain. They listen, hold your hand, rub your back, offer you comfort and acknowledge that the situation stinks. They offer compassion and kindness. They try to relate to your feelings of pain. They don't rush in to fix you or try to solve the problem. And they don't make the situation about them.

When I work with students, there is often confusion about the terms pity, sympathy and empathy. Let's

---

32 OK, all right

clarify so you can better understand what empathy is and isn't.

PITY

Pity is more about the discomfort of the person expressing it than comforting the pain of the person on the receiving end of it. It is feeling sad for someone you feel sorry for or look down on. It implies superiority and that the person receiving pity should be better off. Pity suggests a situation could be different, "if only ..." Pity nearly always makes the individual feel worse about their situation. It may even make them believe there is something wrong with them and lead to feelings of self-doubt and shame. It doesn't make them feel better.

SYMPATHY

Sympathy is also about the person expressing it and their feelings rather than supporting the person receiving it. It's a desire to see someone happier or better off because their current situation makes others uncomfortable. While sympathy can be positive and is more helpful than pity, it is still lacking. It is connecting with someone's situation, not their pain or darkness. Sympathetic people often share stories of similar situations to try to make the person in pain feel better, which is a way for the sympathetic person to avoid discomfort.

EMPATHY

Empathy doesn't require you to feel someone else's emotions. It means acknowledging them. It is truly about the person who is hurting, not the person who is expressing empathy. It connects you with the person in pain exactly where they are, not from where you are or where you wish they were. It is a way of letting someone know, "This is not OK, but you will be OK. I will stay with you through this transition."

Expressing empathy can be difficult. It is often a challenge to see what life might be like from another person's point of view. It might be hard to relate to emotions you are not experiencing without making the situation about you. Empathy denies the comforter's ego and goes all-in for the person in need.

Empathy is not about letting someone wallow in their pain or misery and never get beyond it. Empathy is walking side by side with that person on their journey and reminding them they are not alone. It bridges the gap between pain and joy, stagnation[33] and forward motion, darkness and light.

GIVE IT A BEAT

Darkness and pain are uncomfortable. It's human nature to want to rush past it and move toward the light, which feels better. But it's important to experience the in between. Think about a sunrise. As the moon descends, the sun comes up gradually over the horizon. There is a transition from dark to light. If the sun appeared in the sky all at once, it would be jarring to the senses. There would be no gradient of amazing colors. If you don't give it a beat and pause to appreciate the transition, you miss its unique beauty.

Like the sun and moon, give others and yourself time to transition slowly and gently from darkness and pain to light and joy. Strive to be and surround yourself with people who are gentle with you during these transitions—those who provide hope in your darkest hour.

---

33 Inaction, sluggishness

DO THE WORK

Confession time: I have done a lot of personal work in my life to move from a place of sympathy to one of empathy. I used to be a person who responded to a friend's time of darkness by immediately sharing stories I thought would be encouraging. I would try to rush the process and get us both back into the sunshine. I thought it was for the good of my friend. I was wrong.

Now I know the most encouraging thing I can do is to just be present—to see my friend, listen to them, hear them, hold them and let them know it is OK to feel whatever they are feeling. I let my friend know that I am not going anywhere. I acknowledge that what they're going through must be difficult. I tell them I understand it may feel like too much for them to bear alone. I reassure them that even if the transition from dark to light takes longer than expected, we are in it together. The sun always comes up eventually. And man, is the sunrise beautiful!

Understanding the differences between pity, sympathy and empathy is important. Learning to deliver on those differences is critical.

POSSIBILITY

I often tell the students I work with, "Start believing in your possibility, not your probability." In the words of one of my favorite "Star Wars" heroes, Hans Solo, "Never tell me the odds!"

Sometimes—oftentimes—in life, you have to be extraordinarily brave in order to get something done. If Olympians or surgeons spent time thinking about the odds of becoming the best in their disciplines, they probably wouldn't become gold medal-winning athletes or world-renowned physicians. So instead, they spend their time believing in and training for their possibility, rather than focusing on their probability.

It's true, you need a huge amount of self-confidence and bravery to accomplish some things. But you also need to learn to believe in your long-term possibilities so they can become remotely achievable. Yet it's human nature to spend time getting discouraged by the odds against you rather than giving yourself credit for what you have already accomplished. Then you spend even less time believing your goal is possible and that you will simply find a way to accomplish it.

There are certain people who seem like they were born with more self-confidence and swagger than others. These people tend to end up in sales, aviation, art, entertainment, medical and legal professions. Many of them launch or work for start-up businesses. These fields require the people who work in them to have an exorbitant[34] amount of trust in their possibility, not their probability. And they must be willing to work hard to achieve that possibility, no matter the odds.

I don't believe these people were born with more natural self-confidence. They might have some inherent[35] traits like curiosity and outgoingness that helped them build confidence. But their confidence likely comes mainly from the skills they developed along the way.

Perhaps they never lost the boldness they possessed as a 5-year-old who insisted on wearing a Batman cape and a tiara in public because they didn't give a second thought to anyone judging or questioning them. Perhaps these adults got comfortable keeping their courageous kid self front and center. They may have even faked their way through it and might feel like impostors. The

---

34 Enormous, extreme
35 Natural, ingrained

reality is that each of these people did it a different way—their way. They beat the odds, making it to the top of their field, one way or the other.

While only a small percentage of athletes go on to be Olympic champions, everyone can believe in their possibilities. You can learn to focus on your possibilities more and trust that you have what it takes to reach your goals. After all, Han Solo made the Kessel Run in less than 12 parsecs[36] because he never believed the odds.

---

36 Unit of distance used in astronomy

BADASSERY

A quick note about the word badassery: People who know me are sometimes surprised that I use it. Swearing is not part of my everyday vernacular.[37] But sometimes a word, even one some consider a swear word, is the right word. I believe it is in this case. If you don't like it, insert your own word that means someone with awe-inspiring confidence and strength.

There is a great quote from award-winning TV producer, screenwriter and author Shonda Rhimes: "I try hard to think I am special, to be in love with myself. I strive for badassery." She has achieved this goal in the eyes of many. She is the force behind Shondaland, which created hit shows like "Grey's Anatomy," "Private Practice," "Scandal," "How to Get Away With Murder," "Station 19" and "Bridgerton"—to name a few. Her book, "Year of Yes," is filled with confidence-boosting strategies and inspiration.

Badassery is the result of having major inner

---

37 Vocabulary, expression

strength. It lives in people who have a high level of self-love, self-trust and self-security—otherwise known as confidence. I encourage you to strive for your own level of badassery. Here are the ingredients needed to achieve it:

1. Self-love
2. Self-trust
3. Self-security
4. Swagger

The first three ingredients have already been covered in this book. So what's next? Learning to swagger.

Some believe swagger is actually false bravado.[38] I disagree. If you want to swagger or sashay, I encourage you to do so—all day long. There is nothing wrong with holding your head high and walking with confidence. Walk the way you want, and don't let anyone tell you you can't.

Swagger and sashay are fun words to say and even more fun to do. If you don't know what I'm talking about or haven't done it, practice walking this way in your own space. One of my favorite scenes in the movie "Miss Congeniality" is watching Sandra Bullock learn to walk differently. I would be a hopeless case if I had

---

38 Bravery, courage

to learn to walk in heels like her. No thank you! But I encourage you to find your confident walk and use it.

Something amazing happens when you walk tall past people. They smile. They say, "Wow, you look happy" or "You are clearly having a good time." People like to see other people's joy. They feel comfortable around confident people. It gives them the courage to be confident as well.

Sometimes the students I work with are afraid to walk tall. Instead, they shrink themselves. Please, don't make yourself smaller. Don't try to become invisible. Don't worry about walking, looking and acting like anyone else. It might not seem like it now, but you are only here for a short time. So what if the world takes notice of you? They need to notice you. You are a badass!

Strive every day for badassery—to be someone who exudes self-love, self-trust and self-security, all swirled together with swagger.

PART TWO:
CONFIDENCE THREATS

"Belonging is being somewhere where you want
to be, and they want you."

—Dr. Brené Brown

ELEPHANT

There is a giant elephant in the room right now. It goes by many names and often tries to hide, but it's hard for something as big as an elephant to go undetected. The elephant in the room is anxiety. Anxiety is feeling uneasy, nervous and worried about events in life.

I have worked with hundreds of students over the past decade and have never met a more anxious generation than yours. In many ways, it is the fault of the adults of my generation. I apologize on behalf of all of us and our well-meaning intentions gone awry.[39] I have said to my own adult children, "We weren't perfect. We tried our best, and someday you will work it out with your therapist."

Most humans struggle with some level of anxiety. It is part of life. I am not giving you a formal diagnosis, labeling or judging you. I am sharing my story with the hope of relieving you of pain.

---

39 Wrong, astray

I relate to the weight of anxiety. I have GAD[40] and PTSD.[41] I am not ashamed; I know it is not my fault. My brain simply created an unhealthy way to cope with the trauma and stress I've experienced in my life. Now in my 40s, I am finally doing the hard emotional work required to heal.

This deep work often requires professional help, which is beyond the scope[42] of this book. In order to become more confident, it's important to deal with any underlying anxiety. I know it can be scary, but if you can name what you are experiencing and accept it, then you can start to do the work to heal it.

Why is it so important to deal with anxiety? As you've learned, self-trust is one of the main ingredients to building confidence. Anxiety leads to uncertainty and fear, which are enemies of self-trust. Recognizing and taming the elephant helps you succeed in your confidence journey. If you can, I encourage you to do so. But most importantly, I urge you to stop hiding it, covering it up, or pretending it doesn't exist. An elephant will eventually show itself, and often during the most inopportune time.

Anxiety can show up through catastrophizing, shame and self-doubt.

---

40 Generalized Anxiety Disorder
41 Post Traumatic Stress Disorder
42 Framework, parameters

CATASTROPHIZING

Catastrophizing is living in the worst-case scenario. You assume the worst will happen, even without an honest assessment of the reality of your situation. This often leads to jumping to conclusions and assuming the situation is more dire[43] than it actually is.

In my work, I see young adults catastrophizing on a daily basis. Many of my students are burdened with test anxiety, perfectionism, hopelessness, lack of confidence and fear. I get it. There is a ton of pressure on you every single day—too much really. It can make you feel like you have no choice but to meet certain expectations and play a specific role. With all you have to deal with, how could you not be anxious? How could you not catastrophize?

To get past it, sometimes you need to let your mind go there for a moment to know you can survive. But it needs to stop. If you find yourself catastrophizing, use these effective strategies to deal with it:

1. Play out the worst-case scenario in your mind.
   - Let your thoughts run wild.
2. Quickly come up with three opposing stories.
   - Ask yourself, "Yes, but what if?"

---

43 Drastic, critical

3. Compare the stories.
    *   Focus on the actual likelihood of all scenarios.
4. Remind yourself you always survive.
    *   Humans are resilient and things are rarely as
        bad as we fear.
5. Let it go.
    *   Sing "Let It Go" from "Frozen," if it helps.

In the moment, it can be hard to see through what you believe is impending[44] doom. So much of anxiety is just wasted energy spent worrying about possible futures that never come to pass. As Obi-Wan Kenobi said, "You have done that yourself." In other words, you aren't aware you are catastrophizing. You aren't trying to do it to yourself. So why does it keep happening to you? The answer is rooted in shame.

SHAME

When I see adults shaming young adults, intentionally or unintentionally, it makes my blood boil. In my work, I have heard and witnessed horror stories from students who have been shamed about their weaknesses by peers, parents, teachers, coaches and even friends.

---

44 Approaching, hovering

I mentioned Dr. Brené Brown earlier. She is a researcher and expert on shame and her tools are some of the best. She defines shame as "the intensely painful feeling or experience of believing that we are flawed and therefore unworthy of love and belonging." She explains how, at its heart, shame is fear of disconnection because of who we are, or something we have done or failed to do. Shame leads us to believe we are unworthy of connecting with others.

Do you ever feel this way? Can you see how dangerous this way of thinking could be? Please stop shaming yourself. You are always worthy of love and belonging. YOU ARE ENOUGH.

I am not a social scientist with years of experience like Dr. Brown, so I encourage you to dive more deeply into her books, "Daring Greatly" or "The Gifts of Imperfection." In both, she offers practical advice on how to combat shame and rewrite the negative self-talk that furthers shame. Her Gremlin Ninja Warrior Training for building shame resilience includes tools for recognizing shame, practicing awareness of it, owning and sharing your story and communicating feelings and needs.

The bottom line is this: You may not be able to

control others who try to shame you, but you can control how you react to it. You can also control how you treat yourself, so be careful not to shame yourself. Never forget that you're the narrator and protagonist[45] of your story. That means you can tell it in a positive light. You can receive the love you deserve and find a community where you belong.

SELF-DOUBT

The young adults I work with don't trust themselves enough. This is common for people your age, especially as you are growing and changing. The irony[46] is that many grown-ups believe young adults are overly confident. Some of you may be brazen[47] in your actions, but I'm referring to the feelings that underlie your actions.

If you've never experienced self-doubt, you may not even need this book. A whole separate book could be written about you! The reality is that most humans experience self-doubt. It would not be possible to keep developing without it. Some self-doubt is good and healthy and propels you forward. When it turns into constantly second-guessing yourself, it becomes counterproductive.

---

45 Hero, lead character
46 Twist, oddity
47 Bold, shameless

Have you ever found yourself rehashing a previous conversation over and over in your mind? Have you wondered if you said the right thing? Do you find yourself ruminating[48] about whether someone took something you said or did the wrong way? Does this self-doubting tend to happen when it's time to do homework or go to bed? This is not uncommon.

Oftentimes, when you fear being judged, it means you are judging yourself. I remind you once again, YOU ARE ENOUGH. And you were enough during that moment you are replaying in your head. You can't go back and relive it. If there is something you really need to fix or change, it will come up again in real life, not just in your mind. You can face it and deal with it then. But until then, all self-doubt does is kill your confidence.

Remember, confidence is about self-trust, self-love and self-security. You can't build real confidence in yourself when you are constantly beating yourself up. You can't trust yourself when you doubt every choice, action and word that comes out of your mouth. When self-doubt pops up, use these strategies to combat it:

1. Own your story.
    •   Accept what happened, the way it happened.

---

48 Considering, pondering

2. Stop ruminating.
   - Don't keep replaying the event in question in your head.
3. Find the good in the event and go forward.
   - Highlight what you did right, learn from it and move on.

TYING IT TOGETHER

This chapter could have been three separate chapters. Because catastrophizing, shame and self-doubt are all tied closely together, it's important to read and think about them that way. This will likely be a chapter you refer back to.

You may have heard the saying, "How do you eat an elephant? One bite at a time." The same is true with dealing with anxiety. As it comes up, take it one bite at a time. One day at a time. One rewritten catastrophe at a time. One battle with the shame gremlins at a time. One more dual against self-doubt at a time. And don't forget, YOU ARE ENOUGH.

SMILE

Glennon Doyle is an author and activist. A quote in her book "Untamed" refers to Leonardo da Vinci's painting, the Mona Lisa. You probably know about the Mona Lisa—it's the most famous painting in the world. It hangs on the walls of the Louvre Museum behind bulletproof glass and thousands of visitors view it every day. For centuries, people have discussed Mona Lisa's gaze and smile (or lack of smile) in the painting. In her book, Glennon Doyle imagines how the Mona Lisa might respond to having her expression critiqued: "Don't tell me to smile, I will not be pleasant. You will see the truth, you will see my life is beautiful and brutal."

I have always loved the image of Mona Lisa and her half smile. It's as if she could be letting everyone in on a little secret about her life, but she's not ready or willing to give it away. When I read the quote in "Untamed," it made perfect sense. And I don't think there could be a better description of what it's like to be a young adult—beautiful and brutal. It may describe you or your life.

Each day, you get to choose how to respond to your life circumstances. Yet, all too often, young adults are told how to respond: "Fake it till you make it." "Just smile and nod." "Be happy." "Man up." "Put your big girl pants on." "Turn that frown upside down."

This advice, often offered by well-intentioned adults, can sting and leave you feeling inadequate and alone. I am not going to tell you to smile, pretend or fake anything. Some days you cannot turn a frown upside down, and you don't have to. You don't need to hide your true feelings to make someone else feel more comfortable.

It is important to keep your emotions in perspective. What you feel is valid and important. Emotions are informational but they are not always trustworthy. Allowing your emotions to dictate your life and your decisions can be unhealthy. It is OK if you are not content. It is OK if you are unhappy or upset about where you are in this moment. I'm not saying it's OK to wallow in misery or get caught up in a cycle of pessimistic thoughts. That won't help your confidence, your mental health or your emotional well-being. But pretending you are happy to put others at ease is not going to benefit you either. Find your place of truth and then push yourself to do and be better, until you actually feel better.

I have been told on more than one occasion that I have RBF.[49] It doesn't bother me because anyone who knows me knows I am kind, gentle and warm. Plus, I know it's more about the person who perceives my expression (or lack of expression) than it is about me. Don't get me wrong. I am a big fan of smiling and smile often. Smiling can make you feel good, and it can make the people around you feel good too.

Still, everyone has times when they don't want to smile. There are bound to be days when your insides feel turned upside down or when what's happening in the world affects your ability to smile. Let yourself have those days. Someone might get an impression of you based on your expression that isn't exactly who you are. That's OK. You are still you, no matter what others believe about you. It's OK that the world knows your life is made up of both brutal moments and beautiful moments, just like Mona Lisa's.

---

49 Resting bitch face, unfriendly expression

PERFECTION

I shared information about perfection in the first chapter, "You Are Enough," and this chapter is devoted to it entirely. You'll notice a connection between the two.

Perfection is an ideal that does not exist outside of the ideal. Reread that sentence as many times as needed in order to believe it. You may need to stay on this page for a while to let it sink in. Seriously, perfection does not exist. It's a figment of the imagination. If you struggle here, you may need to find a way to rethink and reframe your relationship with perfection.

I am big a fan of GOOD ENOUGH. Based on the work I do, it might surprise you that I am. You would not be holding this book if I needed it to be perfect. It is GOOD ENOUGH by my standards and GOOD ENOUGH to share with the world. A publisher even agreed with me. Is there more I could have written? Yes. Could I have written it differently? Yes. Is anything important missing? Possibly. Does it still have a lot to offer you and the world? Yes. Is it a good representation of the book I had in my brain before it was published? Yes. This book is not perfect, and that is OK. It is more than OK. It is fantastic! Otherwise, it would still be sitting in my brain or on my laptop and not in your hands. More often than not, GOOD ENOUGH is the exact right answer.

Many artists, writers, dancers and performers struggle deeply with perfection. If you identify as one of these, you know what I mean. You have probably had an experience where you see a vision so clearly and beautifully in your head that what ends up coming from it can feel like a meager[50] translation. Artists are often unable to accept the imperfections that come with trying to present an amazing vision to the real world.

The idea of perfection might be important to you because it pushes you to share your beauty and wisdom with the world. But that way of thinking, the need for something to be perfect, means the world will never see any of it—not even your not-so-perfect interpretation. Why not settle for progress? Why not make peace with GOOD ENOUGH when it comes to your art, your education, your work and yourself?

---

50 Skimpy, insufficient

Progress is something most people can get behind. Progress is forward momentum. Progress means something is actually happening. Progress shows discipline. Progress shows growth. Progress is a reward. It truly is!

When I had the idea for this book, it was just a beautiful vision that lived in my head. What brought it to your hands was my disciplined work each day and my ability to know when it was GOOD ENOUGH to hand off to the publisher. When you know something doesn't need to be perfect, you start to believe you can achieve your goals.

When I work with young adults on standardized tests, one of the first things I show them is how many questions they can get wrong on the test and still get a score they are happy with. This baffles many students initially. Then there is a shift in mindset when they realize they don't need to get a perfect score, that they can actually have several wrong answers and still accomplish their goal. This is an example of GOOD ENOUGH in action.

By now you have probably figured out how much I appreciate the word ENOUGH. It was almost the title of this book. These two statements from the first chapter of this book belong here as well:

- I am ENOUGH just as I am.
- I say ENOUGH to anything that feeds my self-doubt.

Sometimes ENOUGH is a positive affirmation and a way of celebrating who you are, exactly as you are. Sometimes ENOUGH is a boundary that needs to be stated loudly, firmly and emphatically[51] to let whoever or whatever is causing your self-doubt know that you mean business.

Later in this book, in the "Confidence Toolbox" section, I provide proven strategies for battling perfectionism. Two tools that work particularly well for moving forward with progress and confidence are "Let It Go" and "Chunking."

I know how tempting perfection is. I know how hard it is to accept that GOOD ENOUGH is actually GOOD ENOUGH. But it is one of the most important gifts you can give yourself on your confidence journey and in your life overall.

---

51 Assuredly, decisively

SHOULD

There are certain words or phrases I wish I could abolish[52] from the English language. Near the top of my list is "should." Here's what I believe: It's time to stop shoulding on yourself.

I am a recovering should addict. I used to beat myself up with shoulds. I should have done this. I should do that. I should, I should, I should. Eventually, I found myself in a dark and disgusting place, underneath a big pile of should. Then one day I woke up and promised myself I would no longer should on myself. It wasn't easy. But I have been able to stick with it, and it has been worth it. I am happier and healthier because of it.

Have you ever stopped to think about what should means? Here is one definition: SHOULD is just COULD with SHAME attached.

---

52 Prohibit, cancel

In the "Elephant" chapter of this book, you learned about shame and how to fight against it. The best place to start is not willingly inviting it into your life. The next time you find yourself saying, "I should," pause and replace it with one of the following:

- I could …
- I get to …
- I find value in …

Remind yourself that the decision is always yours. You could. You have the opportunity to. But you may not actually have to. Sometimes, there truly are things you have to do. But there are probably far fewer have-tos than you have led yourself to believe. Do not let guilt enter the equation.

As you now know, confidence is made up of self-trust, self-love and self-security. Shoulding on yourself is counterproductive to all of these. Remember, Dr. Brené Brown's definition of shame is "the intensely painful feeling or experience of believing that we are flawed and therefore unworthy of love and belonging." When you focus on should, you attach the belief that you are flawed to your choice. There is no need to do this. YOU ARE ENOUGH, just as you are, no matter what. Make the decision not to attach SHAME to COULD, to not SHOULD on yourself.

DISRESPECT

Ted Geisel (better known as Dr. Seuss) once explained that his success was due in part to being annoyed by something and deciding to change it. That's partly why you are holding this book in your hands today. I got annoyed and finally decided to do something about it. What annoyed me? Disrespect toward young adults.

Disrespect is not an acceptable or normal way to treat another human being, no matter their age. I have witnessed far too much disrespect toward young adults from adults. I have watched the way the world treats and judges you. I have seen it happen with my own children, the students I work with and young people I don't know.

I work with young adults out in the "wild"—in coffee shops, libraries, co-working spaces. I have observed disrespect toward them in nearly every form. Disrespect can sometimes be subtle, like a lack of attention or care, not making eye contact, a change in tone of voice or moving on too quickly. Other times the offending adult is blazingly obvious in their disrespect: talking down, being dismissive or flat out ignoring the young adult. It saddens me when I see a student accept disrespect as "the way it is" or at a loss about what they can do to change it.

You've probably had your own experience feeling disrespected. Perhaps a doctor or store clerk talked to your parents instead of speaking directly to you. Or there may have been an adult who crossed the street or looked away to avoid talking to you instead of smiling, waving or interacting.

Meanwhile, respect is constantly demanded of you. I get how unfair it is. You are required to show respect even when you feel disrespected. This is a life lesson you will carry with you forever. You will meet many disrespectful people, and you will show them kindness and respect anyway. Do not let others' disrespect toward you make you think less of yourself. Don't let it make you bitter, angry or disrespectful.

I taught each of my children to be their own advocate[53] at a very young age. While a parent was usually present when they had one-on-one meetings with a teacher, coach or doctor, our young children

---

53 Champion, spokesperson

were expected to "run" the meetings. The adults in these situations were often surprised, which was initially a surprise to me. And then it became more of a disappointment.

As the parent in these situations, I learned the best trick was redirecting eye contact. When my child spoke to an adult and the adult responded to me instead of the person who addressed them, I looked at my child rather than making eye contact with the adult. This typically sent a signal to engage directly in conversation with my child. It worked, and eventually the adults in my kids' lives started to treat them with more respect.

You can advocate for yourself and demand respectful treatment. Here are some things to keep in mind and try out:

- Write down ahead of time what you need to communicate in the situation.
- Be smart in your timing.
- Be polite but firm in your communication.
- Speak clearly and respectfully.
- Push through anxiety or intimidation with incremental[54] steps and practice.
- Be persistent.

---

54 Additional, increasing

- Remind anyone who speaks over you or for you that you are speaking and would like to finish your comment.
- Practice the confidence strategies in this book.

Of course, not everyone treats young people disrespectfully. Some adults don't realize they are being disrespectful and would probably feel remorseful if they knew they were coming across that way or making you feel less than. I am sorry if you have experienced disrespect from an adult. People of all ages can be poor communicators. That does not make it OK or acceptable, but I believe most people aren't intentionally trying to dismiss or hurt you. It may not take away the sting, and it doesn't take away the reality, but don't forget, there are many people in your life who do respect and admire you.

I often hear from adults that it must be difficult to work with young adults all day. I don't feel that way at all. I think young adults are awesome! I respond by explaining that you are just like adults who deserve a little more grace because you are still learning. We really are all the same. Adult brains are more developed, and we have more experience, but that's simply because we have existed longer. The fact is everyone is still learning. Everyone deserves understanding and forgiveness. Everyone needs room to improve and grow.

One of the promises I made at the beginning of this book was to respect you; hopefully you have felt it. You are a beautiful human, and you deserve respect even when you make mistakes. We are all flawed. We all fall short. Everyone deserves some grace. YOU ARE ENOUGH. You are worthy of respect, kindness and love. Always.

ENTITLED

This chapter might feel different from the others. That's because it is. It addresses humans who go too far and mistake freedom to be themselves, or selfishness or entitlement for confidence. These are the people who tend to justify their actions no matter how they affect those around them.

While writing this book, I received feedback from some adults who read an advance copy that some of its contents could contribute to creating entitled young adults. Specifically, they wondered if this book could lead young people like you to justify selfish behaviors. I thought long and hard about their feedback and took it seriously. And this chapter addresses the concerns head on.

There is a world of difference between healthy self-confidence and entitlement. I believe most of you are mature enough to know the differences are substantial. If you can't see it, you might be slightly overconfident in your personal abilities and rights.

Self-denial, confidence and narcissism exist on a spectrum, and there are entire books written on each of these subjects. This book was written for those of you in the middle, or who tip toward the self-denial end of the spectrum. Confident people take both their own needs and how they may affect others into account. The goal of this book is to help you develop healthy, respectful and loving confidence.

Confidence does not equal self-worship. Confidence isn't entitlement. Confidence does not mean putting yourself above all others. Confidence does not harm others. Those behaviors are characteristics of selfishness, not confidence. It's important to know the difference and stay in the healthy zone.

Nearly everyone has experienced these unhealthy individuals: the self-promoters, those who make everything about them, the people who think the world revolves around them. These individuals tip too far toward the overconfident or narcissistic side of the spectrum. They are not models of healthy self-confidence. Research shows most people with these personality tendencies are some of the least confident among us. They often have very fragile egos that need to be fed. Like the Wizard of Oz, they put on a grandiose show to the world but exist as a fragile individual behind the curtain. If, when you take an honest look at yourself, you see some of yourself that way, you may want to research narcissism. But don't lose hope. It's possible to change this behavior if you put in the work.

If you are having trouble seeing the difference between self-confidence and entitlement, this guide can help you put it into perspective:

Self-Confidence	Entitlement
Rooted in how you view yourself	Rooted in how others view you
Based on self-love	Based on self-worship
Quiet and humble	Arrogant and showy
Owns weaknesses and mistakes	Exaggerates strengths
Works to improve	Makes excuses for behavior
Contagious and builds up others	Toxic and tears down others
Accepts life as is	Believes they are entitled to more

Nothing in this book gives you permission to become an entitled person who does whatever they want, whenever they want. True self-confidence is not believing you are better than anyone or above the rules. That behavior is the exact opposite of true self-confidence.

FITTING IN

Humans have a deep desire for companionship and to feel welcome. Most everyone wants to belong to something or someone. But belonging and fitting in are not the same. In her book, "Braving the Wilderness," Dr. Brené Brown explains the difference: "Belonging is being somewhere where you want to be, and they want you. Fitting in is being somewhere where you really want to be, but they don't care one way or the other."

In young adulthood, many relationships seem to fall into the category of fitting in rather than belonging. This constant pressure to fit in can lead to your confidence taking a hit. When you are required to change yourself to be like everyone else, it is not an act of self-trust, self-love or self-security. Instead, it is putting your trust in the desires and beliefs of someone else.

You are reading this book to learn how to build your confidence. As you've learned, that starts with accepting yourself as you are today. It means genuinely loving yourself the way you deserve to be loved. It means trusting in yourself and your abilities. It means knowing that you have what you need to handle the challenges that come your way. Being confident is not letting someone else decide who you are and what you are capable of. Remember, you're the quarterback and the hero. No one else gets to choose for you.

Even the definition of fitting in is painful: being where you want to be, but no one cares. Ouch! Everyone has experienced this at one time or another. So why keep going back for more? Why try to fit in somewhere you are not wanted and don't get to be yourself? If you've experienced this more than once, chances are it's because you want to feel seen, heard, loved and respected by others. But fitting in doesn't result in any of those things. And as you work on developing confidence through self-love, self-trust and self-security, you will find you are no longer willing to settle for fitting in. You will know you deserve more. You deserve to belong.

If you have ever felt like you truly belonged somewhere, you know how incredible it is. It is empowering when you walk into a room exactly as you are and everyone is happy to see you. It helps you love and trust yourself more and makes you secure in your choices.

Love yourself enough to be yourself. Trust yourself to pick good friends, ones who accept you as you are. When you are true to yourself, treat others with kindness and respect and accept them for who they are, you will find yourself surrounded by other like-minded individuals—those who love and support you through good and hard times. These are the people you want to do life with.

You may also know how alienating it can be to walk into a room and not fit in, to feel like the people there expect you to change to meet their idea of "the norm." You may have been in a situation where you felt like you had to hide or deny parts of yourself to fit in only to realize no one cared anyway. If this has happened to you, it's not because you intended to make yourself feel bad. It just means you lack maturity and have more growing to do.

There is a popular internet meme that says, "Maturity is learning to walk away from people and situations that threaten your peace of mind, self-respect, values, morals, or self-worth." I agree with this wholeheartedly. Don't settle for fitting in. Let go of anyone who tries to change you into something more like them or their unattainable idea of perfect. Give yourself permission to walk away, to find a different room or find a different community. And if you haven't found a place where you feel you truly belong, you can always be the one to build it.

SURVIVAL

My hope for your life is that you are thriving and not just surviving. Too often, young adulthood can feel like a survival of the fittest. But it doesn't have to. I am in my 40s and recently went through a major life transition and period of survival. I realized the effect that living under constant stress and using mainly my survival instincts had on me. It reminded me of the young adults I know who are living in survival mode every day.

Survival mode is an important physiological[55] response to a potentially deadly situation. It's your body's way of preparing for a real threat to your safety (like a lion attack). Your instincts kick in to respond to mortal danger: fight, flee or freeze.

While crucial in dire situations, survival mode is not supposed to become your body's response to everyday stressors. You are not designed to live in a constant state of stress and anxiety. Yet, many young adults today live

---

55 Physical, bodily

exactly that way. Psychologist Robert Leahy reported in the American Psychological Association Journal of Personality and Social Psychology, "The average high school kid today has the same level of anxiety as the average psychiatric patient in the early 1950s." In other words, 70 years ago, people were hospitalized for the level of stress that young adults experience in their daily lives today.

If you're not sure whether you're living in survival mode, here are some indicators. See if any of these statements ring true for you:

1. I am living in a constant state of fight or flight.
2. Everything feels immediate and urgent.
3. I am just trying to get through the day.
4. I am never caught up no matter how much work I get done.
5. I cannot think beyond the next 24 hours.
6. I live in a constant state of reaction.
7. I am not sleeping or eating well.
8. I never feel happy.
9. I feel alone and helpless.
10. I have a hard time asking for help.

How many of these apply to you? Are you surprised by your tally? Are you shocked that these conditions are considered survival mode? You may feel like these are a part of normal life. They are not. Humans are not designed to live this way 24/7.

When you are caught in a cycle of trying to survive, your body is under tremendous physical and emotional pressure. You may experience headaches, muscle tension, stomachaches, bathroom issues and exhaustion. It can feel like you are too tired to get out of bed in the morning. You may not feel like you have the energy or enthusiasm to grab life by the horns and ride it for all its worth—even if you really want to.

Being in a continual state of survival is like swimming in shark infested waters or being caught in a pit of quicksand. Your instincts might be to fight, punch, run or scramble your way out. But that can make things worse. Instead, you've got to learn to ignore your instincts for a bit. Take a moment to sit still and gather your wits. Think about a logical and strategic way to deal with your current predicament. Instead of focusing on the perceived gravity of the situation, focus first on getting yourself to a safe place—physically and emotionally.

Emotional safety is included here because it is often

neglected. From my own experience working with young adults, I have found that the lack of emotional safety is just as much of a threat to your well-being as the lack of physical safety. It can leave you in a constant state of fight or flight, along with a sense of confusion about why you're feeling unsafe when you're not in physical danger. Unless you address both physical and emotional safety, you'll remain in survival mode.

Go back and review the list of survival mode indicators. For the statements you can relate to, what are the reasons you identify with them? Is there someone or something specific that leads you to believe those statements are true for you? Consider what you can control so you can stop operating in survival mode, even if it's taking small steps. This is where change begins. Once you are safe physically and emotionally, you can begin the process of living and thriving.

Here are three strategies that can help you move from surviving to thriving:

1. Be aware of the causes of your survival mode behavior. Acknowledge them, call them by name, write them down and own them.

2. Set firm boundaries to protect yourself from whatever or whomever is contributing to your survival mode.

3. Enforce your boundaries—even and especially when it is hard and you face push-back.

If you find yourself stuck in survival mode, don't lose hope. Your actions influence the direction your life takes, and you can control your actions. Always remember there is some aspect of your life you can control. Even if it's something small, like making your bed, start there. Small steps can take you from surviving to thriving.

Important: If you are in any sort of immediate physical or emotional danger, please seek professional help. Getting help may mean working with a therapist or another kind of medical professional. Talk to trusted adults right away who can support you in getting to a safe place physically and emotionally.

PART THREE: CONFIDENCE TOOLS

"You always had the power, my dear, you just
had to learn it for yourself."

—Glinda the Good Witch, "The Wizard of Oz"

TOOLBOX OVERVIEW

Now that you have a better understanding of the keys to confidence and what can threaten your confidence, I am going to get more practical. This next section of the book is a collection of additional strategies and tips to help you build and protect your confidence.

Some of these strategies may not resonate with you. If you get to something that doesn't apply to you, in the words of Obi-Wan Kenobi, "These aren't the droids you're looking for. Move along." Some suggestions may seem goofy to you. Others could be game changers for you. You won't know which ones will work for you until you try them.

When I coach students one-on-one, my goal is to help them find what is already inside of them and bring it to the surface. After working together for many weeks, some students say they hear my voice in their heads, nudging them toward the answers. At some point, one of my clients suggested that I hand out rubber bracelets imprinted with the phrase "WWKS?" ("What would Kellie say?") as a reminder of what my students have learned during our time together. Today, I gift each of my clients with a teal "WWKS?" bracelet in our final session working together.

The reality is, there is nothing magical about the phrase, the bracelet or the tools in this toolbox. You may remember the scene with Dorothy and Glinda the Good Witch at the end of "The Wizard of Oz," where Glinda reminds Dorothy that finding her way was never about the ruby slippers: "You always had the power, my dear, you just had to learn it for yourself." That is the secret of this book, and in many ways, life. You were born with everything you need. It is up to you to find your inner confidence and harness it. These tools can help you tap into the confidence that lives inside you.

This section contains proven tools that have been used again and again by my students. Certain tools are designed to accomplish specific tasks. Just as using a hammer on a screw or a screwdriver on a nail won't have positive results, using the right tool for the job is important in building confidence. It can make things go smoother and faster. There are four categories: top-shelf tools, self-love tools, self-trust tools and self-security tools. Some tools fit into more than one category, but they are listed under the one they most closely align with.

TOP-SHELF TOOLS

These are your go-to tools, the ones you'll use over and over. My top-shelf choices may not end up being yours, but they are the ones I have recommended the most to students.

SELF-LOVE TOOLS

These tools help you learn to accept and love yourself as the person you are now and the person you have committed to becoming. They also help you stay positive during life's challenges.

SELF-TRUST TOOLS

These tools support you in filtering and separating truth from fiction and learning to trust your own understanding and beliefs. Some have odd names. Still, I encourage you to give them a chance.

SELF-SECURITY TOOLS

When you need to be reminded that "You've got this" or "You can handle this yourself," these tools are useful. They help you become more secure in the knowledge that you are capable and competent, just as you are.

As a longtime educator, I have learned that while lessons may start with a teacher or coach, they always finish with the student. That means it's up to you to use these tools as a springboard. Make them your own, keep what works and let go of what doesn't. Let these suggestions inspire and encourage you. Don't let them limit you. My hope is that you will find some practical strategies to help you on your confidence journey.

TOP-SHELF TOOLS

"I'm never going back, the past is in the past ...
Let it go, let it go."

—Elsa Anne Martin, "Frozen"

CHUNKING

Every day, I work with students on reaching big goals by breaking them down into several small goals. Whether tackling the college admissions and application process, improving test scores, turning in assignments on time, reading comprehension, ADHD management or building confidence, the process is the same. I call it "chunking."

Let's say you have to read really complex, wordy and boring text. You may feel overwhelmed. This is natural. The first step is to break the text into manageable parts. Look only at the first paragraph or the first sentence. Get a grasp on what is in front of you. Start small. You may not make it past the first sentence or two, but continue one chunk at a time until you understand it.

Find a way to make it sticky in your brain. You could highlight words, make a list of keywords or reword phrases in a way that makes more sense to you. Then move on, one chunk at a time. It might take longer than you want it to. You will eventually find a rhythm to it. You will start to master it. You can't rush through certain things and expect good results.

The point is to start by limiting your focus to one small, manageable and achievable goal. No goal is too small. When done this way, you gain more confidence as you complete each small goal. Repeat this process as often as needed.

If you find yourself frustrated, maybe your goal is too big. Or you may need to try a different goal first. Be patient with yourself. The Great Wall of China's first section took over 26 years to be built, but it still stands today. You are working on building self-trust, self-love and self-security one chunk at a time. One day you will be standing on top of your own Great Wall of Confidence!

DOORWAYS

Have you ever thought about how many doors you walk through in a single day? Think about where you are reading this and where you might go next. You will probably walk through between two and four doors to get there. Now add up the number of doors in a day. It is a lot!

What do doors have to do with confidence? Swimming phenom Michael Phelps once shared in an interview that he gave himself positive affirmations each time he walked through a doorway. This was at his coach Bob Bowman's advice.

While I never had the honor of coaching Michael Phelps, I have seen success with my own students who have used this strategy. You may not remember to say something you like about yourself every time you walk through a door. But simply thinking about it can help you make a habit of it.

Don't worry about how your affirmation may sound to you, just start somewhere. It can be as simple as "I don't suck at math," "I can add well" or "I am getting better at math every day." Eventually, you will get to a point where you compliment yourself like the champion you are. Even Michael Phelps, who is considered the most-decorated Olympian of all time, needs to remind himself how great he is sometimes.

Remember what I shared in the "Just Be" chapter about 10-year-olds feeling free to be themselves? Self-doubt tends to creep in during your early teens. It doesn't happen overnight. It happens gradually. That means it can take a while to rebuild your confidence. Be patient with yourself. When saying something positive about yourself, it helps to be specific about an area of confidence you need to work on.

Don't beat yourself up or allow self-doubt to bring you to dark places. Instead, develop a pattern of thinking that affirms who you are and who you are becoming. Develop the habit of positive self-talk. Talk to yourself the way you would talk to someone you love and respect. Start by doing it every time you walk through a doorway.

WEIGHT TRAINING

Weak muscles, whether physical, emotional or intellectual, can lead to a confidence crisis. When you feel weak, you feel vulnerable, which leads to self-doubt and an inability to trust yourself. It can even make you feel unworthy of love. What's an effective way to strengthen weak muscles? Start a weight training routine.

If you have ever weight trained, you know it has to be approached strategically. You need a plan, equipment and, if possible, a spotter and a trainer. You don't start by lifting the heaviest weight on the first day. You probably aren't ready for it today, but keep working and you will be one day.

Whenever I recommend a weight training program for a student, I start from their current level of strength. We start with light weights and few repetitions. Then, as they gain strength, we either add weight or add repetitions—rarely both at the same time. We gradually build on both until they reach their goals.

This is the best way to approach building your confidence as well. Start small, with something easy, an area where you believe you can succeed. Add a bit more weight. Tackle something you're less sure of. Build up that weaker muscle by adding a few more reps.

The most common weight training I do with students is related to reading comprehension. Many of my students hate reading. (Maybe not you since you've made it this far!) When I help a student with reading challenges, I start somewhere between five and 15 minutes a day of reading for five days a week. You can do anything for five minutes, and almost anything for 15 minutes. Some of my students are surprised that I rarely ask them to go more than 20 minutes a day and max out at 30 minutes a day—and 30 minutes is rare.

The point is not the length of time or level of difficulty. The way to build stronger muscles is through consistency and a routine you can actually stick with. The primary reason people give up, or believe they have failed, is that they tried to accomplish something unrealistic, got discouraged and quit. Intensity is not important here. Consistency is.

Whichever area of confidence you need to work on today, make a plan, start with light weights, do a few reps and celebrate your success. Repeat this process, adding weights and/or reps until you reach your goal. Like actual weight training, confidence building is largely about the process.

20-MINUTE TIMERS

dislike cleaning my house. My entire family would vouch for me. From this aversion, the "20-minute power clean" was born. I set a timer for 20 minutes, blast my favorite music and clean until the timer goes off. Then I set another 20 minutes on the timer to do whatever I want. When that timer goes off, I switch back to a work timer and repeat the process until the house is clean—often in much less time than I anticipated.

Timers can be a tremendous confidence booster. It is amazing how much you can get done in just 20 minutes and how quickly the time can pass. Sometimes, I will take a picture before I start and after I am done so I can see and take pride in how much I accomplished in such a short period of time.

Timers also give you a goal. You've got to beat the clock, to do the thing before the buzzer goes off. If you are an athlete who is driven by timing (a swimmer, runner, skier, basketball player), you can probably relate. You do timed drills to discover your natural pace, your race pace, your threshold pace and the point of your fail training. All of this helps your confidence in the short term and your performance in the long run. My sweet spot is 20 minutes, but when you start out, yours might be 10 minutes. Find your natural pace and your tolerance to discover your own sweet spot and work within it.

The key to making this strategy work is to stick with it. Set the timer and don't quit until it goes off. Really engage, work hard and throw yourself fully into the task at hand. Then set your leisure timer and stop when it goes off. You will be amazed at how much you get done and the boost in your confidence.

LET IT GO!

This top shelf tool comes from the movie "Frozen." You may have just started singing the song in your head. Or you might be rolling your eyes. Hang in there with me for a minute. I use this tool with students who lack confidence in math, but it can help improve your confidence in many different situations.

Let's say you are working on a section of hard math problems that is causing self-doubt. Having witnessed this on many occasions, I can tell you what happens next: deep sighing, playing with hair, bouncing legs, tapping pens, slumping shoulders, looking at clocks, negative self-talk. After a few tough questions in a row, you might bow your head and sink into your chair, shoulders looking like someone put an anvil[56] on your back, your confidence quickly slipping away. None of this actually helps you solve math problems, and it's not a demonstration of self-trust, self-love or self-security.

---

56 Heavy iron block

When you feel defeated, picture the scene in "Frozen" when Elsa finally decides she is going to let everything go. She is strong and powerful. She trusts and loves herself. She believes in her abilities. As the story goes on, Elsa begins to transform what she and others once saw as weaknesses into strengths. She takes care of things on her terms. She does what makes sense for her, not anyone else.

You may be wondering what this has to do with confidence. Everything! If you approach things like difficult math problems with Elsa's attitude rather than falling back on self-doubt, your confidence is going to increase. The next time you face something difficult, imagine telling yourself "Let it go!" Skip the problem that has you stuck and move on to the next. Do you have to get every single math problem correct? Probably not. Let go of should.

Telling yourself "Let it go!" works for all sorts of challenges, not just math problems. Next time you need to move past something difficult, try singing Elsa's theme song in your head. Remind yourself you are in control, and you don't need to be perfect. YOU ARE ENOUGH. Think about how happy Elsa is when she finally trusts in herself—her innate[57] goodness, her

---

57 Natural, inborn

strengths, her abilities. She exudes self-trust, self-love and self-security. She radiates confidence. You can do the same.

WHAT'S NEXT?

After watching all seven seasons of "The West Wing" (my favorite TV show), and hearing President Jed Bartlett use the phrase "What's next?" so articulately[58], I decided those words would appear on my headstone someday. (I know, it's a little ironic.)

"What's next?" conveys a powerful message: Got it. Let's move on. It is a succinct and polite way of saying there is no need to belabor a certain point. It expresses a willingness to go forward and a sense of adventure. It exudes confidence and control.

While coaching students, I often say, "What's next?" I say this when I know they've got something under control and it's time to move on to the next task. This show of faith in them and their abilities helps boost their confidence. When my students adopt this phrase and relay it back to me, it communicates and builds their confidence as well.

---

58 Assuredly, decisively

You may relate more to Ariana Grande's, "Thank you. Next." If so, use that. But it's important to note that "What's next?" is not meant to be dismissive or sarcastic. It's intended to capture the confidence you gained from one success and bring it forward to the next.

Try communicating "What's next?" with positivity and consistency. Do it over and over and it will help you build confidence while showing others how self-assured you are. It will communicate you're proud of what you've accomplished and looking forward to what's next.

TA-DAS

Do you love to-do lists or hate them? Do you have a hard time keeping track of what you have and have not completed? Do you like the feeling of looking back on your accomplishments?

I had a love/hate relationship with to-do lists. There was a time when I would write things down on my to-do after I had done them so I could feel the satisfaction of crossing them off. Apparently, I needed a little boost of dopamine.[59] Then I heard about "ta-das." On that day, I freed myself from to-dos and now I celebrate ta-das.

A ta-da list is written after you complete a task instead of before. It can be as long as you want. You can include the smallest of details if it helps.

Remember how I dislike cleaning my house? I keep a ta-da list as I do it. Seeing that list grow makes me feel better and keeps me motivated. It helps me realize how much I have already accomplished, rather than

---

59 Brain chemical that makes you feel good

focusing on all there is yet to be done. It may seem like a simple mindset shift, and it is. But it can have a big impact. When you focus on and celebrate what you have already done well, it creates forward momentum. When you look at a mile long to-do list and you cross one item off, you can become discouraged.

What you have completed may not be on your original to-do list and that's OK. Sometimes life has other plans for you. Other things needed to get done first. This does not make you a failure. It makes you human. By relieving yourself of the shame of a to-do list and celebrating your victories with a ta-da list, you focus on the good.

Your ta-da list could be as simple as a list you write on a sheet of paper or in your phone. I like mine to be colorful and fun. So I use Post-Its—color-coded because that's how my brain works. As I complete a task, I write it on a Post-It and stick it on a sheet of paper.

I also keep a second sheet of paper that I think of as a home for repetitive tasks (the ones I usually perform every week). I write those on Post-Its in advance and stick them to the second sheet. When I complete one of those tasks, I move the Post-It to my ta-da list. I tell myself that they are reminders and not to-dos, and I am careful not to should myself.

There is more than one way to make a ta-da list. I encourage you to come up with a creative way to create yours based on your unique needs. Remember, the goal is to celebrate what you've accomplished rather than focus on what you have yet to do.

SELF-LOVE TOOLS

"No one can make you feel inferior without your consent."

—Eleanor Roosevelt

OWN THE MORNING

Many successful people say the key to their success is their morning routine. I agree. I believe if you can manage to own your morning, you are on your way to owning your day. When you own your day, you are on your way to owning your week, month and year.

The single greatest contributor to my successful days is having a consistent morning routine. Over the years, my morning routine has been long, it has been short, and it has included many different habits. It has evolved to match the needs of whatever stage of life I'm in. The key is having an intentional plan and following it.

What works for me probably won't work as well for you. You are a different person with different needs, responsibilities, goals and timelines. There is no magical morning routine anyone can prescribe for you. But there is an exercise you can do to help you create your own custom routine.

Start by writing down your current routine, even if what you do doesn't feel intentional. You probably get up around the same time and do certain things. Even just getting dressed and out the door in the morning is a routine. Write down what you do daily over the course of a week. Look for the common actions and the order in which you do them. After a week, review your list and decide what you want and need to keep and what you don't. You can also reorder the things you do in a way you prefer to do them. Then start practicing this daily routine.

The next step is thinking about new habits you'd like to incorporate into your daily routine. Gradually add things to your list, one at a time. It is easier to develop a new habit if you attach it to an old habit—something you've been doing a long time. Be careful not to add more than one new habit at a time or you might find yourself overwhelmed, abandoning your routine altogether. Be patient. Habits take time to develop. Consistency is the key.

I incorporate my previous day's ta-da list into my morning routine. I review and celebrate what I accomplished. It helps me start each day off with positive energy.

Here are some ideas for your morning routine.

None of these are required. I don't recommend trying every single item on this list all at once. It certainly isn't comprehensive; rather, it's a simple list to get you started:

Breakfast	Positive smells
Caffeination	Read
Daily reminders	Self-care
Exercise	Self-grooming
Gratitude practice	Spiritual practice
Medication	Stretch
Meditation	Sunshine
Positive music	Water

When your morning routine becomes ingrained, you will appreciate the consistency and probably miss it on days it gets interrupted.

I am intentional about making my morning routine something I do just for myself. It is sacred to me. No emails, no texts, no meeting other obligations. It is my time to ground myself and prepare for the day. The demands of the rest of the day will come soon enough. Prioritize yourself before you have to face all the rest of your obligations. Own your morning.

DANCE BREAK

The University of Texas in Dallas is known for its headphone dance parties. Students gather together in public wearing headphones, and each student dances to their own music. Clearly the university recognizes its audience includes introverts with eclectic[60] tastes. I could get into that kind of dance party!

It takes guts to put yourself out there without caring what anyone else thinks about what you're doing with your body. Since no one else can hear what's in your headphones, they don't know whether your rhythm or moves match the music. But that's the beauty of it! Others have no idea what is streaming from your headphones. This is a great metaphor for confidence. You can never really know what is happening inside of someone else or the reasons they do what they do.

I love to dance. A few times a day, I take a dance break to boost both my energy and my confidence. I do it alone, in the privacy of my office or home. I take the

60 Diverse, wide-ranging

William Watson Purkey quote, "Dance like nobody's watching" literally. Try it for yourself and see how you feel.

Start with one song. Play it loud and dance to it alone. For the entire song, let your body move however it wants. Smile and release your tension. If you need to, play different songs that relay a few different moods until you find the ones that feel good. My current go-to dance break song is "Sour Cherry" by The Kills.

Take a dance break when you feel down, are low on energy or have been sitting too long. Take a dance break when someone is annoying you, or you need a break from your homework. Much of this book was written with dance breaks in between chapters. Dance breaks can help you feel confident, refreshed and ready to tackle whatever is next.

Maybe dancing feels too goofy for you. Perhaps a run, walk, yoga or lifting weights might be a better option. The idea here is to do something physical. It doesn't need to take long. Just give yourself freedom to move your body in a way that helps you feel good about yourself.

SOUNDTRACKS

Many students I work with use music as a motivator. Maybe you do the same. Your generation is fortunate to have easier access to music than mine had and the ability to make custom playlists with just a few clicks.

Each year, I make a playlist that includes my favorite songs from that year and name it my current age. When I look back at those playlists, I get a good sense of my state of mind and confidence, year by year.

My immediate family has been creating an ongoing playlist together for more than a year. It started as a month-long project and is now more than 25 hours of music. It spans the musical tastes of a 12-year-old up through the favorites of her grandfather in his 60s. We use it to lift up and encourage each other. And though we are scattered across the country, it makes us feel closer to one another. Some families have photo albums; we have a shared soundtrack.

While these playlists are fun, listening to a year's worth of music is not always the best way to enjoy it. I break down my personal favorites into different themed playlists. If you already do this, you know exactly how a particular mix of songs can change your mood and thoughts.

I encourage you to make a specific confidence boost playlist. I'm lyrically driven, so the songs on my confidence boost playlist made the cut based on the messages they relay. You likely have songs that evoke certain emotions and motivate you. Include those in your playlist.

I nearly always have music playing. I have come to think of the playlists that accompany me throughout my life like the soundtrack to a movie. I am intentional in my music choices. The songs feed my spirit, influence my thoughts, enhance my moods and speak to my body. Last year, according to Spotify, my music aura was "positive vibes and empowerment." Do you know your music aura? You might not use Spotify, but you probably have an idea of what your music aura is.

You may have heard a saying about how you are shaped by the five people you spend the most time with. Similarly, the music you spend the most time with becomes part of you. Use it as a confidence tool. Create a playlist that makes you want to swagger and take dance breaks.

COLOR POPS

There was a time when I blended into the background, wearing mostly black, dark blues and beiges. Then I decided to start being more colorfully me. I switched to bright teals, light blues and purples. When I did, a funny thing happened. Not only did adding more color to my life bring me joy and happiness, but I also felt more confident.

Now I use what I call color pops to express myself. I drive a teal Jeep Wrangler. I wear colorful clothing. I paint my nails bright colors. I write with colored pens. I brainstorm with colorful Post-Its.

As it turns out, there's science behind how humans feel about certain colors. Sir Isaac Newton, the scientist who discovered the laws of gravity and motion and invented calculus, also developed the color wheel. Then, in the early 1900s, a psychiatrist named Carl Jung studied the effects of color on the human brain. He eventually came up with a form of therapy that helped his patients express themselves with color. This color psychology is still used today, in everything from developing products to advertising.

Here are some examples of how color affects the brain: The color red is associated with energy and passion. Orange is connected to playfulness, enthusiasm and positivity. Lighter shades of blue represent peace and gentleness. Darker blues are associated with strength and dependability. Green typically has a calming effect.

There are a lot of colors in this crayon box of life. Do you have a favorite? Which ones makes you feel happy and confident? Try adding some color pops to your life. Surround yourself with colors that create positive emotions for you!

SURROGATE

In the "Quarterback" chapter, you learned one of the keys to confidence is surrounding yourself with supportive people. Here is another way to look at it.

You may want to be strong and confident, and you might want to be able to do it all by yourself, but sometimes you can't. Sometimes you have to be willing to accept the help of others until you can do it on your own and be OK with that decision.

Surrogate mothers carry babies for others who either cannot become pregnant or cannot maintain a viable[61] pregnancy. Surrogate mothers (true heroes in my opinion) help families get started or grow. They generously give of themselves and give hope for the future to those they are assisting.

In your confidence journey, you may need a surrogate from time to time—a special person who can carry confidence for you.

For example, coaches like me act as surrogates for

---

61 Possible, feasible

confidence. When I meet students for the first time, many feel beaten down and have lost faith in themselves and their abilities. Part of my job is to carry their confidence for them as they learn to become confident themselves. I believe there is nothing as rewarding in life as watching an individual's burgeoning[62] confidence.

A surrogate's job is done when the pregnancy ends. The family starts a new journey, thankful for the help they received during a time when they felt vulnerable. The surrogate may develop a bond and a connection to the child they carried and their family, but part of their gift is stepping back and letting go. Same goes for confidence surrogates.

In addition to coaches, parents, teachers and friends can all be surrogates who carry your confidence and give you hope when you need it. Even if you want to be able to do it on your own, be gentle and patient with yourself. Be open to a surrogate. Give yourself the support and time you need to develop and grow into a confident person.

Perhaps you have had surrogates in your life and eventually discovered you have this confidence thing figured out. Ask yourself if it is your turn to help

---

62 Growing, blossoming

another. Even if you don't feel ready to lead or teach, could you show someone else that you believe in them until they are able to start believing in themselves?

Maybe you haven't had a surrogate in your life because you haven't needed one. Maybe you have been confident enough to grow alone. If this sounds like you, could you help someone else grow? Could you carry confidence and hope for them until they can do it themselves?

If you see yourself in either of the last two paragraphs, I encourage to pay it forward and become a surrogate to someone in need. Like me, you might discover that watching someone's confidence blossom is one of your favorite things.

SELF-TRUST TOOLS

"I have not failed. I've just found 10,000 ways that won't work."

—Thomas Edison

COIN FLIPS

When your self-trust is low, you are prone to second-guessing yourself and self-doubt. It can result in taking an inordinate[63] amount of time to make up your mind. You might seek the opinions of several other people to help you make a decision. Or you may rehash each decision you make over and over.

If you find yourself doing this, an easy way to make a decision is with a coin flip. Seriously. Get a coin, call heads or tails, and flip it. But rather than going with the outcome the coin reveals (for example, heads you attend an event and tails you don't), go with your immediate reaction. Did you groan when the coin landed on tails and it meant missing the event? Or did your heart sink when the coin landed on heads because it meant attending the event? In other words, base your decision on your gut reaction to the reveal. Were you pleased by the result? Was it what you were hoping

---

63 Irrational, unreasonable

for? Or were you disappointed? That, my friend, is your answer.

My own children have made some major life decisions this way, including where to pursue their education. Was I comfortable with them making these big decisions with the flip of a coin? Yes! This tool for decision-making is not about random luck. It is not about odds. Flipping a coin and acknowledging how you feel about the way it lands simply forces you to be decisive and go with what your gut already knows.

A lack of confidence can prevent you from making the choice you knew was right all along. Learning to trust yourself takes time, but coin flips can help you get there a bit faster. Start by flipping a coin to help you make decisions with little significance to see how it feels. Then move on to flipping a coin when you have bigger choices to make. Eventually, you will learn to trust yourself and you will no longer need a coin.

AUTOPSIES

This chapter is not about what to do. It's about what not to do. In her book, "Big Magic," author Elizabeth Gilbert says, "You don't need to conduct autopsies on your disasters." In other words, don't rehash your mistakes.

An autopsy involves dissecting a body to find the cause and manner of death. It is not meant to undo what's already been done. And despite what crime TV shows and movies depict, autopsies are rare and used only when absolutely necessary.

Cutting a mistake open after it has happened and examining it over and over in your mind isn't going to change the circumstances. Revisiting it only causes you to relive the pain, worry and cast doubt on yourself. It zaps your self-love and self-confidence.

When I see young adults conducting autopsies on their mistakes, it is almost never a problem that warrants that level of dissection. It is simply something they wished had a different outcome.

Some of my students—the ones with an anxiety elephant sitting on their chest—don't even wait until they have made a mistake to conduct an autopsy. They might be pleased with the outcome of something and still worry about what they could have done differently. Either way, what is done is done. Move on to what's next.

If you made a mistake that needs rectifying[64], fess up to it. Accept it and apologize if needed. Be gentle with yourself. Forgive yourself. Do better next time, and keep going forward. But stay out of the autopsy lab. Better yet, don't step foot in there in the first place.

---

64 Improving, bettering

BOUNCE FORWARD

I have never liked the phrase "bounce back." Why go back when you can forge ahead? Life is about progress, momentum and forward motion. Bouncing back puts you behind. Losing ground is certainly not going to help your confidence.

As you face disappointments in life, think about how you will bounce forward, not back. Think of these experiences not as failures, but as learning opportunities. Thomas Edison said about his challenges while creating the light bulb, "I have not failed. I've just found 10,000 ways that won't work."

Thomas Edison was a genius. His U.S. patents[65] are responsible for every item that uses electricity. He created the motion picture industry, the recording industry and the X-ray machine. He operated on four basic principles that he credits to his mother: Experience the world. Never stop learning. Learn with

---

65 Government protected invention rights

your head and your hands. And never get discouraged when you fail.

I doubt Thomas Edison would have liked the phrase bounce back either. Sometimes in your journey, your progress will be slow, maybe even so incremental that you don't feel it. Don't get discouraged. Just keep bouncing forward.

FACE IT

In many aspects of life, when you put in an effort and do the work, you get the results you deserve. When you have confidence in yourself, you can trust and believe you've earned the good results you get.

However, entitlement and the expectation of big rewards with little effort are the opposite of confidence. Do not be tempted by or fall into the trap of the often-used phrase, "Fake it 'til you make it." After all, the definition of fake in this case is "forge or counterfeit something." While those using this phrase may have good intentions, the philosophy can have dark and dangerous downsides.

If you fake something, you haven't earned it. Pretending that you've put in the work when you haven't is not actually going to get you the desired outcome.

Think about it this way instead: "Face it 'til you make it." It is a reminder that putting in the work and facing hard things is required if you want to get through them. You have to keep going to achieve results, even if you feel like giving up. There are certainly benefits to believing you deserve positive results. There are benefits to imagining you have achieved whatever outcome you desire. But ultimately, those results and outcomes must be earned and not faked.

Athletes who put in the required (and often extra) time and give their best effort know they are better trained than those in lanes next to them. This is why they have a genuine sense of confidence in their ability to win. They aren't betting on random luck or raw talent. They made multiple deposits in the bank of discipline and hard work, and now they can make their withdrawals.

This is one of the reasons Olympians are so exciting to watch. They know they deserve to be there, and they know they deserve to win. At this level, sportsmanship is rarely in question. Elite athletes know that while they deserve to win, their opponents are also worthy. They know sometimes they will win and sometimes they will lose, and it doesn't shake their confidence.

"Face it 'til you make it" in your confidence journey. Trust that when you have done the work, you will get the results you deserve.

GLITTER JAR

Thoughts and emotions can sometimes cloud your judgment and get in the way of your confidence. There will be many times in your life when you need to keep them in check. A glitter jar can help you do so.

I first learned about glitter jars reading Lisa Damour's book, "Under Pressure," which I highly recommend. She learned about them from a guidance counselor in Texas. It is a sealed clear jar with glitter, glue and water inside (you can find the recipe online). It can be used in a variety of different ways. I keep one on my desk and use it whenever I need to calm my mind.

When your insides are topsy-turvy—if you are feeling stressed, anxious, confused, angry—shake your glitter jar. Shake it as hard and for as long as you want or need to. Then set it down in front of you. As the glitter moves around in the liquid, imagine that what is happening in the jar is what's happening in your brain.

The flakes of glitter are your thoughts and emotions, making your brain murky.

Many young adults (and adults for that matter) struggle to let their glitter settle. You may try to make decisions during a swirl of unruly emotions and chaotic thoughts. In those moments, you don't have the ability to see the truth of your reality. When you wait for the glitter to settle, you can see through the jar again. What remains are facts and clarity.

Like glitter, thoughts and emotions can be sparkly, colorful and beautiful, and they can capture your attention. But they can also be difficult to contain and clean up. There might be days when you need to shake your glitter jar and wait for the pieces to settle several times before addressing a problem. A glitter jar can help you to be more aware of how much your thoughts and emotions are affecting your confidence and your ability to objectively understand reality.

COMPOST PILE

I admire the "mind palace" technique used by Sherlock Holmes in the television series. If you have never heard of it, the mind palace is his technique for storing and organizing memories and important facts with a story that connects them. I am not gifted enough to have a mind palace. My brain doesn't work that way. Mine functions more like a compost pile.

If you have ever composted, you know it is messy and smelly, and it can be hard to believe that waste is ever going to become a place where plants can grow and thrive. And yet, it does. This is how I think of my brain—a depository for thoughts and ideas that will eventually turn into something special. I just keep throwing more on the pile, mixing it up and creating an environment where seeds of ideas can be planted and grow into amazing things.

Mind palaces and compost piles both help build self-trust and self-confidence. When you are able to recall, access and utilize the wisdom and lessons of your past, you trust yourself more. When you trust yourself more, you grow more confident.

Having a compost pile takes some of the pressure off. It is OK if you don't know whether a piece of seemingly random information that is in your head today will be useful tomorrow—or ever. Instead of throwing it in the trash, toss it onto the compost pile, walk away and let it sit. Turn your compost every so often, and one day that random fact may rise to the top as a fertilized and fully fleshed-out[66] idea that is ready to pursue. Many of the quotes in this book were ones I threw into my compost pile. I walked away, and years later, this book came out of it!

You might not have a Sherlock Holmes-level brain. I don't either. That is OK. Find a way to contain your compost outside of your head. I keep a little notebook with me to jot down phrases or ideas that I may not look at again for years. Siri takes all sorts of random notes for me that no one could make sense of but me. Compost piles do not need to be neat and tidy places. They are meant to be contained collections of what might otherwise seem to be refuse.[67]

---

66 Nearly complete
67 Waste, trash

LEVEL UP

Building confidence is a lot like playing a video game where you strive to continue leveling up so you can achieve the next goal.

When you start at a new video game level, it might not seem too difficult at first. You get the lay of the land, discover your mission, and find new tools. Things may be going well, when suddenly, and often without warning, it gets more difficult. You wonder if you can handle this level. You have to work harder, run faster, use more tools and develop more skills. You fail—a few times. But you keep playing, ignore the odds, find a way to level up and start the process all over again.

Each failure teaches you which path not to follow, provides new ideas to consider and guides you toward a different approach. You look back at your progress to figure out where you went off the rails and how you can prevent it from happening again.

As you reach the highest level, things might seem impossible, or at least improbable. You may get stuck. After you have tried everything you can imagine, it's time to reach out to others who have been there, done that, like gamers do. Or you could search for information and watch videos online. Just don't give up.

Getting good at video games takes practice and tenacity.[68] Getting to the end of each level comes with the reward of a new and more interesting level to explore. The more you play certain video games, the more your trust in your abilities grows. The same is true with building confidence. The more your self-trust grows, the more confident you become.

Think of your confidence journey as a video game and keep striving to level up. Keep trying new things, don't give up and enjoy the journey. And don't forget to celebrate each new level.

---

68 Determination, courage

ROAR

Katy Perry's song, "Roar," is one of my all-time favorites and seems to fit many life situations. It tells a story I think many people can relate to about keeping quiet, either because you were told to, or because you don't want to risk upsetting anyone. In the video, she takes viewers on a journey through the jungle where she must fend for herself and adapt to survive. She finds her strength and newfound confidence and conquers obstacles that get in her way. Ultimately, she finds her voice and isn't afraid to use it.

Do you ever find yourself being quiet when there is something you want to say? If you develop a pattern of it for too long, you may start to forget what you believe or know to be true about yourself. You might adopt what others think is true about you instead. Remember what you learned from the "Just Be" chapter at the beginning of this book? Never stop being to start seeming. Letting others decide what's best for you isn't worth it, and it won't keep you any safer in the jungle.

When you don't stand up for yourself, other people or causes you believe in, you stand for nothing. You give away your power and lose your voice when you allow others to make decisions and speak for you. If this is something you struggle with, it is time to reclaim your voice. And you may need to do it the way a lion does it—with an actual roar.

Go outside to an open field or in nature and roar as loud as you can. Or roar behind a closed door in a room in your house. Feel how empowering it is to roar. Where you do it is not as important as simply doing it. Do it whenever you need to reclaim your voice. Remember how powerful your roar can be when you find yourself keeping quiet instead of speaking up.

Reclaim your voice. It's there for good reason. It allows you to fulfill your purpose and gives you confidence. It reminds others that your thoughts and ideas matter and deserve to be heard and considered.

SELF-SECURITY TOOLS

"'No' is a complete sentence."

—Anne Lamott

GRATITUDE

In addition to boosting confidence, practicing gratitude is beneficial to humans in many ways. It helps increase empathy and decrease aggression. It improves physical and mental well-being. It helps foster relationships. It leads to better sleep.

During the COVID-19 lockdown, I started a daily gratitude practice. It is easy to do. Start each day with three things you are thankful for from the day before. Write them down. It doesn't matter where or how you write them. What matters is taking time to reflect on the good in your life.

You may want to keep it in a five-year journal, with one page for each day. When you're done, you can look back on your daily reflections over a span of five years. You can purchase a specific five-year journal if you like, but nothing fancy is required. You could use a notebook or even keep a daily note on your phone if you prefer doing things digitally. Either way, this simple act can change your perspective for the day and your outlook on your life.

If you aren't sure what you are thankful for, here are a few general things to consider:

A new day	Having opportunities
Being alive	Family, friends, pets
Experiencing emotions	Nature

I encourage you to be more specific. Instead of focusing on things, try focusing on experiences. Once you've done this exercise for a while, you will see patterns in your entries and discover who and what you are most thankful for. It can help you become more confident in the choices you are making and the life you are building. This practice can even help you organize your life and make space for and prioritize what you are most grateful for.

FIVE IN FIVE

In her book "Girl Stop Apologizing," Rachel Hollis recommends creating a list of 10 goals to accomplish in 10 years. That seemed out of reach for me, but the book did inspire me to identify five goals for the next five years. This feels more attainable for me, and it may feel more doable for you as well.

Start by imagining your life five years from now. If it helps, close your eyes and actually picture yourself in your mind. Where are you? What do your surroundings look like? Are others with you? Who are the people with you? What would you like to have accomplished by then? What kind of life are you leading? This is the time to dream big. Write each thing down in the form of a goal, and as if it came true and has already happened. You could start your list with, "It's the year (five years from now) and ..." Here are some examples:

It's the year 2030 and ...

1.   I am living in Seattle, Washington.
2.   I am a graduate of the Seattle Film Institute.
3.   I am working as a digital video producer.
4.   I have three golden retrievers.
5.   I am planning to launch my own business.

Once you have five goals, write five bullet points with specific actions you can take to reach that goal. What are the steps you can take over the next five years to get there? For example, actions to help meet a goal of living in Seattle might include visiting family members who live nearby for a tour and researching video producer jobs in the area.

This can be a powerful activity and keep you focused on what you really want out of life. It is also a confidence booster. When you visualize your future self and see your goals in front of you, you start to believe you can and will achieve them.

If five goals in five years feels intimidating, start with three in three, or even one in one. The idea is to imagine yourself in the future and start working toward that vision today.

SUPERHERO

I'd like you to try an experiment right now. Stand up tall, face forward, plant your feet firmly on the floor, tilt up your head and chin and put your hands on your hips. Now stand like this for 30 seconds to a minute. Think about how you feel.

This is a superhero stance, a high power pose. Body language research conducted by Amy Cuddy at Harvard University shows that high power poses, which are open and relaxed, actually make you feel powerful. This type of posture makes you want to take risks and take action. It even reduces stress and anxiety. Can you believe that just standing a certain way can increase your confidence? It does! I am not a scientist, so I don't know what exactly goes on in the brain to make this happen. But I have seen it work for many of my students. So even if you are skeptical, stand up and try it.

Superheroes lead with their strengths. They are confident. When you stand like a superhero, you show the world you are prepared and ready for what may come your way. When you exude a sense of confidence, others are more likely to trust and believe in you and your abilities.

Many public speakers stand with a power pose on stage as they begin to deliver a speech or presentation. Starting this way not only captures the audience's attention, but it can also ease your nerves and help you think more clearly.

Standing like a superhero is by no means magic. To build true confidence, you need to prepare and work at it. But the strong stance is a confidence booster. Why not give it a whirl?

TAKE UP SPACE

Have you ever watched a confident person walk down the street? You probably noticed the way they held their head high or their strong posture. Perhaps you observed how aware of their surroundings they were, or how others naturally made space for them. Moving through the world this way is not obnoxious, offensive, or unkind to others. It is simply someone taking up the space they deserve.

The students I work with know that I take up space. My work surfaces and the chairs nearby are typically covered with my books, notes, bags and supplies. I use whatever leg room I need. I never try to make myself small.

Young adults are often criticized for being "too much" or for taking up too much space. I have worked with thousands of young people and have never experienced one of my students trying to take up more space than they need. I have not observed them trying to intimidate others with the spread of their limbs or take control of a room. I have only witnessed young people trying to find a way to get comfortable with their growing bodies, and burgeoning confidence. What I have seen is humans merely trying to find the space they need to fit into the world around them. I commend this!

No matter your gender, I encourage you to take up the space you need. Go ahead and get comfortable without encroaching[69] on the space of those around you. Arrange your work, your stuff and yourself in a way that suits your needs. Allow others around you to do the same. And then don't give it a second thought.

For some of you, the idea of taking up space might be tough. You may not have tried it, or you may think you don't have the right to do so. You deserve the space you need. Building self-security requires making yourself seen and taking up space.

---

69 Intruding, invading

COMPLIMENTS

When you believe you are capable and competent and someone pays you a compliment, what do you do? You accept it. You simply express your gratitude to the person giving you the compliment and smile if you happen to feel like smiling.

The key to accepting a compliment is learning to say thank you and nothing more. When you receive a compliment and reply, "Thanks, but ..." or demur[70], you are not being self-secure or kind to yourself or the person offering the compliment. You are second-guessing yourself. You're sending a message that you don't think highly of yourself or your actions and you don't want others to either. You are also questioning someone else's judgment and intentions.

Confident people don't say, "Thanks, but I'm really not that great." Take the compliment. Believe it; trust it; let yourself feel good about it. Someone else believes you deserve it.

---

70 Hesitate, waver

Don't mistake making yourself small for being humble. True humility is a quiet, honest acceptance of your strengths. It doesn't mean denying them when they are noticed.

On the flip side, don't use a compliment as an opportunity to brag or draw attention to your strengths in an arrogant way. When it comes to accepting a compliment, less is more.

Giving a compliment to someone else is also an easy way to make you both feel good. Don't force it or fake it. When there is something you appreciate or like, simply compliment the individual and move on. Complimenting others not only boosts their confidence, but it lifts yours as well.

NO

Author Anne Lamott is known for her quote, "'No' is a complete sentence." I have worked over 40 years to develop "no" as a complete sentence. Now it is one of my favorite sentences to use.

There will be many situations throughout your life when it is OK for your answer to simply be "no." You do not owe anyone an explanation. So often, "no" is truly enough.

Most people have been conditioned to justify their "no." But when you say more, you are opening yourself up for a debate. The person you've said "no" to may think your answer is not definite. My rule for "no" is the same as my rule for holes—when you are in one, stop digging. Better yet, don't start digging in the first place. Say "no" and move along.

You may notice people are startled when you start using "no" as a complete sentence. They may wait for what comes next—because something nearly always does. Get comfortable with the awkward silence. Wait it out. You have said all you need to say. Don't follow up your "no" with an "I'm sorry." No apology is required. Be firm in your answer and your limits.

"No" is about boundaries and respect. It's important to know, communicate and honor your own boundaries. Then require others to respect them. If you find yourself in a relationship where "no" is continually questioned or disrespected, it is probably not a healthy relationship.

When needed for emphasis, you could say "Hell no!" I reserve this for situations when I strongly disagree or dislike something. This lets the other person know I am adamant[71] about my "no" and works for me because I so rarely swear. But before using a "hell no," be certain it is appropriate and needed. It will rarely ever be justified with a parent, educator or coach. Most often with these adults, a simple "no" will suffice.[72]

---

71 Insistent, determined
72 Be sufficient, meet the requirement

SUPERPOWERS

I work with a wide range of neurodiverse[73] young adults. I help students with ADD, ADHD, anxiety, perfectionism, dyslexia[74], dysgraphia[75] and OCD[76]—to name a few. Note that I use the term neurodiverse and not disabled. This is both an intentional choice and the truth. These are not disabilities, and individuals with these conditions are not necessarily at a disadvantage. Rather, these students face unique challenges. And they also possess unique strengths. They simply have brains that work outside the typical box. Society may have labeled these traits as disadvantages, but I want you to see them for what they really are: superpowers.

Think about Bruce Banner in "The Hulk." In the beginning, he has very little control over what triggers him and transforms him into The Hulk. As his story progresses, he learns how to control both his mental and physical strengths to his advantage.

---

73 Different ways of thinking, learning, processing and behaving
74 Reading challenges
75 Writing challenges
76 Obsessive Compulsive Disorder

If you have the gift of ADD or ADHD, I highly recommend Dale Archer's book, "The ADHD Advantage." Yes, I said gift. You may have been told your condition is a problem, but you are not flawed. You are amazing. Dr. Banner saw his condition as a problem until he learned how to leverage it.

Many individuals I know with ADD and ADHD have the ability to focus at a ninja level on things that interest them. These ninjas, however, may also need help managing tasks they find less interesting.

One of the skills many individuals with dyslexia possess is logic. They have an ability to think outside the box and come up with creative solutions to problems. They might also need more time to complete certain tasks.

People with dysgraphia might not be great spellers, but they tend to be great listeners and have strong memorization skills.

These conditions come with challenges, but they are all gifts too. Learn to accept your skills for what they are and find a way to harness them. Manage both the advantages and the downsides. Eventually, you will see them as the superpowers they are.

GRAVEYARDS

Graveyards are typically a final resting place. I recommend keeping a graveyard of your own. No, I am not encouraging the collection of bodies. Rather, you may need a final resting place where you can leave your skeletons (unwanted experiences and thoughts) for good.

My graveyard is a small notebook I carry with me. When someone or something really bothers me, I write it down. I look through my notes again later that day or week. After some time has passed, the things I wrote down usually no longer matter to me. I can easily let them go. Every now and then, there is an item that remains stubborn. I allow myself to hold on to it for up to a month. Then I commit to letting it go. Either way, the unwanted experiences and thoughts I've written down are in their final resting place.

I am not suggesting that keeping a graveyard is a replacement for asking for help for bigger problems.

If you are facing anything significant, please seek the support of a trusted adult. However, it is important for you to learn how to handle life's minor challenges on your own. The graveyard approach puts you in control. It allows you to acknowledge an issue, work through it if you need to and say goodbye to it.

Don't live your life in a graveyard surrounded by ghosts. As you become more secure in yourself, it becomes much easier to leave negative people, experiences and emotions behind.

CONCLUSION

Thank you for taking this journey with me. I appreciate you being honest with yourself from the start and accepting yourself for who you are, as well as the person you are becoming. I am rooting for you as you continue this journey.

Remember, the keys to confidence are self-trust, self-love and self-security. Self-trust is believing in yourself. It's recognizing you are an amazing and capable human being. You can rely on yourself to make good decisions and do great things. Self-love is learning to love yourself, right now, exactly as you are. It is not worrying about being perfect or pushing yourself so hard. Self-security is being secure with yourself. It's knowing you have everything you need inside you and don't need to lean on others to feel certain, safe or secure.

As you work on building your confidence, your progress will be threatened by the messages the world sends you and your own internal struggles like anxiety and perfectionism. Recognizing confidence threats will allow you to address them. Using the tools in the confidence toolbox will empower you to overcome them.

I hope you will continue to use the information and tools in this book to continue to build your self-love, self-trust and self-security. Keep being the amazing person you are, with even more confidence.

Let's end our time together the same way we started. Take a few deep breaths, close your eyes and see yourself for who you are right here and right now. Never forget, YOU ARE ENOUGH, exactly as you are.

In friendship,
Kellie

P.S. I'd love to send you a teal "WWKS?" bracelet! Send me an email at kellie@uconfidence.com.

P.P.S. For more information about my coaching services, visit my website at www.uconfidence.com.

RECOMMENDED READING

"The ADHD Advantage" by Dale Archer
"Braving the Wilderness" by Dr. Brené Brown
"Daring Greatly" by Dr. Brené Brown
"The Gifts of Imperfection" by Dr. Brené Brown
"Rising Strong" by Dr. Brené Brown
"Set Boundaries, Find Peace" by Nedra Glover Tawwab
"Under Pressure" by Lisa Demour
"Year of Yes" by Shonda Rhimes

ACKNOWLEDGMENTS

This book would not exist without my former clients, students and parents. You inspired, challenged and pushed me to grow into the coach I am today. Throughout our time together, I developed many of the strategies and lessons I share in the pages of this book. Thank you.

To Deepali Roth, Julie Burton and ModernWell, Jan Nickels and everyone at OffiCenters, thank you for helping me realize that UConfidence is a substantial business, seeing the true value of the work I am doing, and providing me with spaces for my students, even during the COVID pandemic.

To Chris Olsen, Leslie Lagerstrom and the entire team at Publish Her, I could not ask for a more supportive and encouraging team. With all the publishers available, I am so glad we found each other. You believed in me, made my work better, and helped me bring it to the world. Thank you.

To my student advisory board, Aspen Chambon, Ashwin Wilson, Jax Surprise, Madison O'Callaghan, Rohit Wilson, Kyla Borgendale, Elise Bargman, Parker Will, Sydney Gremmels, Lauren Taylor and Sean Vigil, you helped me stay true to my audience and to myself and made every aspect of my book better.

To my parent advisory board, Esra O'Callaghan, Suzie O'Gorman, Melissa Wargin, Kris Foudray, Kristin Fisher, Melissa Mark, Susan Chione, Renee Van Dusen, Keri Jackson, Nicole Rasmussen, Kristi Biel and Mindy Heine, your support as friends and former clients has been so valuable. Your willingness to provide a never-ending sounding board helped bring this book to life in a way that makes it valuable to both young adults and parents.

To my mother, Kathleen O'Callaghan, who gave me my first blank journal and encouraged me to write. To my father, Jim O'Callaghan, who has always been my number one fan, cheerleader and supporter, and the best father a girl could ask for. To my brothers Jim, Shaun and Tim, who know me better than most and still love me after all these years. To the wonderful O'Callaghan clan, you raised me to know that anything is possible regardless of gender or starting point, to stand up for what I believe in, and to break through invisible ceilings. Above all, you showed me "family first forever." Thank you to the Pepe, Kelly and Cripe families who believed in me. To Billy Cripe, for always believing I had a book in me and for two decades as my best friend. Thank you all for your support throughout the years.

Finally, to Keltan, Cael and Kessel, I am thankful for each of you beyond words. Being your mother has been my greatest journey. You have inspired and encouraged me every day. You have loved me through the ups and downs. Keltan, you read and edited my manuscript over and over until it was finished. Cael, you encouraged me to keep going and reminded me to smile and laugh more. Kessel, you were by my side throughout the entire process. You put up with my constant questions, requests and 5 a.m. alarms, and you kept me real. Now I have the privilege of watching each of you make your way confidently through the world and live lives you are proud of. Nothing could make me prouder. You are loved and cherished always. You are more than enough and you are truly amazing, exactly as you are.

With gratitude,
Kellie

ABOUT THE AUTHOR

Kellie O'Callaghan has more than 20 years of experience in academic advising and education and is the owner of UConfidence, a successful academic coaching business. Kellie's dedicated no-nonsense approach and easy rapport with high school and college students have earned her the admiration and trust of thousands of young adults and their families. Every day, she sees how their academic and personal successes are positively influenced by her tried-and-true approach to improving confidence. She offers them a powerful and needed message: YOU ARE ENOUGH.

Kellie has a master's degree in communication and lives in Minnesota and South Carolina. She has parented and launched three young adults of her own.